NIGERIA: POLITICS AND POLICIES FOR NATIONAL DEVELOPMENT

Chima Imoh, PhD.

(Public Policy and Leadership)

Heritage Publishing Company

Houston, United States of America

Heritage Publishing Company,
7447 Harwin Drive,
Houston, TX 77036.
Copyright © 2014 by Heritage Publishing
Company.

Library of Congress control Number: 2014915708

Imoh, Chima

Nigeria: Politics and Policies for national
Development/Chima Imoh
P.cm.-(politics, policies and development)

ISBN-978-0985479244
1. Politics-policies-national development.
2.   Nigeria-democracy-private property rights
    practices. I. Title. II. Series

Printed in the United States of America

PREFACE

Decades after the advent of the much-acclaimed globalization, huge differences still exist in levels of development among nations. Some nations that should attract foreign capital and investment have failed even when they possess high potentials for growth and development. Obviously, organizations and investors wishing to invest in a country are always concerned about such issues as the political, economic, and regulatory conditions that underscore the repatriation of profits, the risks of political instability, as well as the fiscal policies of the country. A new entrant to a foreign market, therefore, has to understand the potential threats to market growth, as well as the general business environment.

Although, the effects of globalization on the fledgling economies of the developing nations have been subject of intense debates; less contentious are the determinants of Foreign Direct Investment (FDI) into the developing economies. Most countries in the sub-Saharan Africa have not been successful in attracting foreign investment; and when some of these countries do attract foreign investors, they do so mostly only in the areas of their mineral resources as is the case with Nigeria. Examining national development as it pertains to Nigeria entails exploring such issues as the internal constraints to development; the trends of flow of foreign direct investments into Nigeria, as well as the underlying constraints to FDI inflows to the country.

Arguments have, however, been made that the inflow of FDI into such Sub-Saharan African countries as Nigeria has not created the anticipated benefits of economic growth; nor the transfer for technology and managerial skills. Some scholars have posited that the reason is that such conditions as higher-level economic and human capital development must be in place before the benefits of FDI are derivable.

Public policies have been used as tools for the positioning of national economies into the global supply chain. Some governments in the Sub-Saharan Africa have achieved meaningful outcomes; positioning themselves into global supply chain by setting up Free Trade Zones (FTZ) and Export Processing Zones (EPZ) along the coastal cities in the region.

Like every other, Nigeria's government should be mindful of the need to attract foreign investment into the country. Despite the historical and institutionalized constraints, Nigeria could attract more foreign direct investments by carrying out some systemic reforms. Such countries as Mozambique and Uganda have, for instance, been somewhat successful in improving the inflows of FDI by carrying out policy reforms. To attract more diversified FDI, the governments of Nigeria, must, through public policies, make new and sustainable efforts to improve the investment climates within the country.

In this book, the focus will be on postulating that a combination of favorable investment climates and high level of human capital are required to attract interest of investors. The book, therefore, seeks to examine the linkages between Foreign Direct Investment (FDI), and the public policy environment in Nigeria.

Chima Imoh, PhD.

ABOUT THE AUTHOR

Dr Chima Imoh has a degree in Geodetic Engineering and a master's degree in international management. He has a doctorate degree in Public policy and Administration, specializing in public management and leadership. Dr Imoh is a member of the National Honor Society for Public Affairs and Administration, United States of America. The author has lectured and worked in public institutions in the United States and in Africa. Dr Chima Imoh is the author of three books, *Cultural Competence for Global Management; Policymaking and Development Strategies for Local Governments in Nigeria; and Elections, leadership, and development in Nigeria*. He is also a co-author of the book, *Competency for Public Administration,* edited by Dr Susan T. Gooden and Dr Kris Major.

CONTENTS

PART I

Democracy and its Indicators

Chapter 1

The Indicators of Genuine Democracy

Political regimes are not democratic by claiming so or by merely embracing such institutions of democracy as legislature[1]. Being democratic also means welcoming the existence of opposition parties, and letting them organize and campaign freely against the ruling party. Robert Rotberg had, in *Governance and Leadership in Africa,* argued that under stable democratic systems, opposition parties thrive, elections are free and fair, and ruling parties are sometimes voted out of power[2]. More so, the democratic state holds regular elections, supervised by independent and impartial electoral commissions[3]. A democratic state, therefore, espouses and supports such essential as freedoms of expression, worship, movement, assembly, and from want[4].

Democratic values do not only rest on representation, but also in recognizing and accepting the sovereignty of the people; the protection of the civil and political rights of the citizens; ensuring the political participation of the people; and being politically accountable to the people.

Recognizing and Accepting the Sovereignty of the People

In a democratic state, the sovereignty of the people is upheld, encouraged, and nurtured by creating the right environments for political accountability to the citizens; ensuring political participation of the citizens; protecting the political rights of the citizens; and genuine electoral competition among political contenders. The article 21 of the Universal Declaration of human rights (UDHR) stipulates that political authority should be based on the sovereignty of the people[5]. Ultimately, the government is responsible to the people, and political office holders should be controlled by the people through elections.

The measure of the level of democracy in a country could thus, be assessed on the basis of a regime's recognition and acceptance of the supremacy of the people's sovereignty. The sovereignty of the people could be practiced and assessed through such institutional values as accountability, representation, constraints on executive, and participation[6].

Political accountability

Democracy offers the advantage of rooting public policies in political accountability[7]. This political accountability ensures the responsiveness and accountability of the government to the governed; the transparency of government actions and services; and the accessibility of all to government programs and services.

By generating public accountability, democracies also impose checks on elected officials and policy makers[8]. This is because; the public demand for accountability creates incentives for governments to adopt policies that are conducive to growth[9]. Moreover, by compelling elected officials to consider the electoral consequences of the behavior, political accountability increases the chances of delivering public goods[10].

The theory of democracy emphasizes that competition between political parties creates and fosters more responsive governance by shepherding elected leaders toward service and accountability. To achieve this, the state and political processes must make it possible for the citizenry to effectively participate in genuine electoral competitions. Electoral competitions in Nigeria have, however, not always attained the levels desirable for elevating the leaders toward the higher ideals of service and accountability.

Protecting Political Rights of Citizens

As the egalitarian democracy theorists argue, more emphasis should be placed on basic rights of the citizens; as the value of democracy lies largely on the protection of the political rights of the citizens; namely, the ability to hold officials accountable or throw them out of office[11]. Protecting these political rights of the citizens requires the institutionalization of an impartial judiciary; as well fearless press and a vibrant civil society.

Political Participation of citizens

Achieving democracy's key element of empowering the citizens entails their active participation through their ability to elect or dismiss their political leaders by means of genuine competitive elections. A robust and healthy democracy is only as possible as the active participation of the citizens in public life[12]. Effective participation requires that citizen would be able to form their own political associations and pressure groups[13].

If, however, the people are to participate in politics, they would need to have some confidence that their individual participation would contribute or make some difference to governance[14]. Article 25 of the International Covenant on Civil and Political Rights (ICCPR) indicates that citizen participation in the public affairs of the state, especially in genuine periodic elections, is fundamental to democracy[15].

Citizen participation is important for a variety of reasons: to promote democracy, build trust, increase transparency, enhance accountability, build social capital, reduce conflict, ascertain priorities, promote legitimacy, and cultivate understanding, or advance fairness, and justice[16]. A key to these political goods is an electorate that is both willing and able to participate in domestic politics. A democratic framework should, therefore, help citizens to participate by debating and resolving their value differences as to reflect consensual views that approximate closely to public interests and good; thereby contributing to the development of the society.

Genuine Electoral Competition

A democratic state would always hold regular elections, supervised by independent and impartial electoral commissions. The repeated holding of genuine competitive elections produces improvements in civil liberties, strengthens civic organizations by giving officeholders some incentive to service[17]. One key mechanism for enforcing the accountability that is inherent in a true democracy is through these periodic conducts of genuine elections.

In genuine electoral systems, the preservation of the integrity of the ballot box as the expressed will of the people should be a fundamental interest of the state. A democratic system cannot, therefore, be considered genuine if the ballot is compromised, or preferences are coerced[18]. To fulfill the fundamental rights to vote or be elected as specified in article 25 of the International Covenant on Civil and Political Rights (ICCPR), the state is required to conduct genuine and periodic elections[19]. Elections are genuine when they are competitive; the will of the voters freely expressed; and votes are counted honestly and accurately. The genuineness of electoral competition can be assessed by virtue of the how open and competitive they are; as well the credibility of the opposition.

(i) **Presence of credible opposition**

A source of political accountability is the level at which existing democratic structures possess real opportunities for alternation of power. This alternation of political power is better assured by the presence of credible opposition. The presence of credible opposition guarantees that there is an alternate government capable and waiting to take over from the incumbent government. This in turn, puts pressure on the ruling government to be responsive and accountable to the citizens.

In the book, *Political Man: The Social Bases on Politics*, Seymour Martin Lipset indicated that the existence of the opposition is in essence, an alternative government; serving as a restraint on the incumbent government[20]. Only an opposition that has the potential to win an election and form a new government can provide a strong external incentive for the incumbent government to act in the interest of the citizens[21]. Political competition, when accompanied by repeated and genuine elections, therefore, generates a credible threat of this replacement[22].

Without the credible threat of replacements through elections, however, elected officials have fewer incentives to provide public goods. In ideal democratic settings, when incumbent governments sense that the opposition is strong and credible enough to take power, they act in ways that would enhance public satisfaction with their activities[23]. It is, therefore, the presence of credible opposition that ushers in accountability.

(ii) Competitiveness of elections

The competitiveness of elections is the extent to which executives are chosen through competitive elections[24]. The defining characteristic of democracy is the regime where high political offices and legislature get elected by means of contested elections in which the political competition is formatted in such a manner the reasonable uncertainties exist with regard to outcomes[25]. This democratic system loses its genuineness if, and whenever the voting system is compromised. A genuine democracy, must, therefore, preserve the integrity of the ballot by preventing its corruption.

(iii) Openness of elections

The openness of elections refers to the extent that all politically active population has an opportunity to attain executive positions through a regulated process[26]. Political activities are hinged on law, becoming more open, and hence increasing democratic consciousness[27]. For the credibility of the process, elections require openness and transparency. Without openness or transparency, therefore, no accountability is possible[28].

Chapter 2

The Advantages of Democracy

A stable democratic state would have competitive elections whose outcomes are uncertain; as well as potentialities for alternation of parties in power. At the minimal level, the people should be able to elect or replace their political leaders through regular, free, and fair elections[1]. The hallmark of an established democracy is, therefore, the ability to resolve the problems of leadership succession by means of elections without turmoil[2].

Democracy as an important component of free government, however, carries certain risks, which, if not checked, could enthrone domination[3]. Such risks include the absence of genuine electoral competition, which, for instance, transformed most of the civilian regimes in Nigeria into electoral dictatorships. The conduct of elections does not mean that they are free and fair[4]. For that reason, free and fair contested elections can be used as the procedural definition of democracy.

Larry Diamond[5], in *The Spirit of Democracy,* had outlined the attributes of democracy as having:
(i) Substantial individual freedom of belief, opinion, speech, publication, broadcast, assembly, demonstration, and petition.

(ii) The freedom of ethnic, religious, racial, minority groups, and even the historically excluded majority groups to practice their religion and culture, as well as participate equally in political and social life.

(iii) The right of all adult citizens to vote and be voted for, as long they meet the age and competency requirements.

(iv) Genuine openness and competition in elections.

(v) Legal equality of all citizens under a rule of law, in which the laws are clear, publicly known, universal, and not retroactive.

(vi) An independent judiciary that neutrally and consistently applies the law; protecting individual and group rights

(vii) The due process of law and freedom of individual from torture, unjustified detention, or interference in their personal lives by the state.

(viii) Institutional checks on the power of elected officials, by independent legislature, court systems, and other autonomous agencies.

(ix) A vibrant press and "civil society" that ensures pluralism in sources of information.

(x) Institutional control of the military and state security apparatus by civilians who are ultimately accountable to the people through elections.

Robert Dahl[6] in, *Who Governs? Democracy and power in the American City*, enumerated the advantages of democracy:

(i) Helping to prevent government by cruel and vicious autocrats.

(ii)   Reducing injustice and increasing political equality among the citizens.

(iii) Offering more rights band opportunities to the citizens

(iv)   Ensuring a broader range of personal freedom

(v)   Helping citizens protect their own fundamental interest

(vi)   Providing maximum opportunities for citizens to exercise freedom of self-determination.

(vii) Guaranteeing citizens some fundamental rights that non-democratic systems do not.

(viii) Providing maximum opportunities for the exercise of moral responsibility

(ix)   Fostering human development more fully than other systems of governance.

(x)   Fostering a relatively high degree of political equality.

In addition, modern representative democracies do not fight wars with each other[7]. Furthermore, countries with democratic governments tend to be more prosperous than those with 'non-democratic' governments[8].

Although, Nigeria has a multiparty electoral system, has significant opposition, and has some space for the civil society and dissenting intellectualism; elections are, however, riddled with fraud. Electoral competition is so constrained and dominated by the domineering power of incumbency that it is difficult to call the system a democracy. Nigeria occupies the ambiguous space between democracy and overt authoritarianism; is classifiable as an electoral authoritarianism.

Chapter 3

Internal factors constraining democracy in Nigeria

Democratic ideals seek to guarantee equality and basic freedom; the empowerment of the citizens, resolution of disagreement through peaceful means, and to enthrone political, social, and renewals without disruption1[1]. The practice of democracy also offers popular control over the elected leaders, equal rights and liberties, political freedom, freedom from wants, upholding the rule of law, justice, and security[2].

Democracy, therefore, means more than regular conduct of elections. A genuine democracy must be able to deliver what the people expect in terms of development and decent governance[3]. Democracy must also provide ongoing means for achieving accountability and responsiveness, as well as making political leadership broadly representative[4].

Unfortunately, Nigeria's democratic practices are grossly deficit. The deficits of Nigeria's democracy include the non-accountability of elected officials, disregard for the rule of law, violations of human rights, and election malpractices. Judged by its key elements, democracy in Nigeria falls short of acceptable standards. The reasons for the low standards of democracy could be many; but the four fundamental problems are: the perversion of democracy, poor democratic culture, fraudulent electoral practices, and the passivity of the electorates.

Perversion of Democracy: Nigeria's Electoral authoritarianism

At the end of military dictatorship in 1999, Nigeria did not transform into a democracy as was popularly thought; but rather transformed into electoral authoritarian regimes that combine democratic and non-democratic characteristics[5]. Steven Levitsky and Lucan Way had in, *Competitive Authoritarianism: The Emergence and Dynamics of Hybrid Regimes in the Post-Cold War Era*, described an electoral authoritarian regime as a political system that combines regular democratic elections with such number of democratic deficits as corruption; and poorly working systems of checks and balances between the executive and legislative branches of government[6].

Although the civilian regimes in Nigeria were set up under formal democratic institutions as multiparty elections; these regimes in reality, only mask their authoritarian domination; are plagued by frequent human rights abuses, disrespect for civil liberties and widespread corruption. Elections are regularly held; but are often bitterly contested and often rigged to favour the incumbent governments, which, control and wield the inherent powers of the state. When these characteristics of authoritarianism are mingled with regular conduct of elections, the resulting political system is nothing but electoral authoritarianism. The so-called democracy in Nigeria is, therefore, nothing but electoral authoritarianism.

Electoral authoritarianism should, therefore, be seen as institutionalized dictatorship that is either absolute one-man rule or where the set pattern for political advancement and leadership does not yield themselves to genuine electoral competition. These practices go against the grains of democracy, whose constructs must be attentive to the system through which people compete for votes.

Poor 'democratic culture'

Most societies have certain types of values, beliefs, and customs that shape how their people think and act politically[7]. There is, however, a human propensity to corner power and monopolize available resources which usually leads to conflicts[8]. Nigeria has for a long time, acquired and nurtured a poor 'democratic culture'. These are the resultant effects of a combination of the traditional culture, colonization, and long years of military rules.

Worse still, colonial governance in Nigeria was in the form of an authoritarian administrative apparatus with a powerful and power-wielding governor at the helm of affairs[9]. To be able to extract and maximize their own interests, the colonizing powers ruled Nigeria with absolute authoritarianism, thereby, exacerbating the already existing traditional authoritarianism cultures. This forceful colonization of Nigeria with the authoritarian imposition of alien systems and conditions contributed to the prevalent poor 'democratic culture' in the society.

The long years of military dictatorship, however,

contributed largely to the prevailing poor "democratic altitude" of the Nigerian citizenry. The political climate of Nigeria has, therefore, for a long time, been marred by the existence of authoritarian and pseudo-democratic regimes[10]. This authoritarian leadership model, has, unfortunately, remained and has continued to contribute to the inhibition of democratic and leadership development in Nigeria.

Fraudulent Electoral practices

A government is not democratic just because its leaders are civilians; but because the road to power and the existing political institutions and the processes of governance are in accord with the working concepts of democracy[11]. Such working concepts of democracy would include free and fair elections, especially the protection of the integrity of the ballot box.

Unfortunately, the electoral processes in Nigeria have remained tainted by manipulations, abuse of state power, the harassment of opposition candidates, and election rigging. For instance, presidential elections are often rigged to favour and actualize the wishes of the incumbent presidents as they wield the instruments of the state[12]. The stakes become even higher in re-elections, when, in order to return the presidents to power, the rigging becomes more extensive[13]. Regrettably, elections in Nigeria only represent the interest of the incumbent political elites rather than the will of the people.

Largely, incumbent presidents, governors, and other

political office holders manipulate elections to remain in office despite their inept governance, poor economic and infrastructure development, low standard of living, and charges of corruption[14]. The incumbent officials, especially the governors and presidents would rather devise more dubious means to hijack the electoral processes than improve their governance. The critical issue is the absence of free and fair elections, with the so-called elected officials not dependent on the electorate to win elections.

Specifically, elected presidents, governors, and elected officials in Nigeria perform poorly and yet the citizens are unable to vote them out because they manipulate the electoral processes through extensive rigging, using the coercive machineries of the state to impose the fraud on the citizens[15].

The absurdity of Nigeria's political situation is that though the people are completely dissatisfied with the performances of the governments, the same dissatisfied people are purported to have continually, at each election cycle renewed the mandates of the inept governments. These political leaders therefore make the people inconsequential to their stay in power; thereby subduing the need for accountability and good leadership.

Obviously, elections in Nigeria are not "contested elections" because there are usually no uncertainties as to the outcomes. Losing the influence of their votes, and hence, no influence over election outcomes, the entire citizenry becomes largely disadvantaged. Democracy is therefore impelled, and loses its value as the stability of the democratic system depends on the effectiveness and legitimacy of the political system.

Disengaged and Passive Electorate

The Nigerian electorate is outstandingly disengaged and passive to the usurpation of its sovereignty. In voting for elected officials, citizens merely yield their sovereignty to such official only on temporarily basis. Such sovereignty is transferred through the electoral ballots and should never be usurped under any circumstances. The Nigerian electorate, however, watches in docility as the politicians forcefully and falsely declare themselves elected in utter disregard of the expressed electoral wishes of the citizens.

A sustainable democratic culture requires that citizens are respectful of government authority but yet, are watchful of it abuses. Essentially, democracies work best when they provide electoral choice, potential for alternation of power, checks on the ruling elites, avenues for exposure and punishments for abuse of power, and legal and political avenues for redressing grievances[16]. These can only be achieved by the reactive and engaged electorate, and not the passive one.

Absence of Genuine Electoral Competition

As the constructs of modern democracy must be attentive to the system through which people compete for votes, a critical issue in Nigeria is the absence of genuine electoral competition. With the political leaders not been dependent on the electorate to win elections, the integrity of the electoral process in Nigeria is really next to nothing.

Obviously, the tendency of political leaders in Nigeria is to stifle and weaken the opposition. Without this credible threat of replacements through genuine electoral competitions, elected officials have fewer incentives to provide public goods. This state of affairs has had adverse effects on the development of the nation. This is because; the fundamental differences in the public welfare disposition and development performance among democratic regimes are essentially outcrops of whether or not electoral competition is restricted.

PART II

Development Models: Analyses

Chapter 4

Analyzing the Modernization Model

Development has been defined as arising from situations when a group of human species in a geographical location acquires the capacities to understand the natural laws that enable them to collectively organize to increase their capacity of production through technological advancement and innovations[1]. Modernization, on the other hand, is a historic process by which agrarian societies transit into industrialized societies[2]. Essentially, modernization is the process of transforming social, economic, and political system into their modern states[3]. The essence of modernization is not only industrialization but also of changes in attitudes, social values, and lifestyles[4]. This model is assumed to be a process with which underdeveloped countries could catch up with the developed countries, not only in the context of economy but also in relations to technology[5].

The modernization model of development had its roots in the problems and experiences of Western societies. Modernization, therefore, encourages a trend of development toward the exploitation of natural resources through the infusion of human capital, financial capital and technology into less developed countries; as the pathway to transit to the modernization, industrialization, and urbanization as in the developed countries[6]. The modernization theorist, therefore, construct the modern society as that in which there is more reliance on inanimate power sources; and that in which goods are mass-produced in continuous and standardized manner[7]. In a modern society, there should be differentiation and functional specialization in governance; with activities based on law[8].

Such early scholars as Gabriel Almond, Wilbert Moore and Cecil Blake used the industrialized western countries as the prototypes for modernization. As modernization was hinged on western concept of development[9]; for practical purposes, modernization is equivalent to westernization[10]. As the concept of modernization grew out of western development, it demands that the developing countries follow the path of development of the developed countries.

Over the years, however, modernization has experienced some infusion from scholars and development economists from the developing countries. Instead of presuming that tradition and modernity are at opposite ends, the new theorists believe that both can coexist and supplement each other[11]. Instead of seeing tradition as an obstacle to the drive toward modernization, the new theorists argue that some traditional elements are capable of exerting positive effects on the drive toward modernization. The new theorists challenge previous assumption that the western pattern of development is the only path to modernization; arguing instead that there are different roads and model to modernization.

Unlike the modernization theorists, the new theorists acknowledge the significance of the external environment on the processes of modernization. The new theorists contended that since modernization model of development had its roots in the problems and experiences of Western societies, it was not adequately equipped to deal with the problems of the unindustrialized societies[12]. These new theorists from the developing countries rejected this western-oriented model, and instead sought to relate development issues to their own countries and regions; giving rise to such theories as the dependency theory and such development models as the Lewis (dual) model.

Chapter 5

Analyzing the Dependency Model

The dependency model of development was meant to address the criticisms leveled against the modernization theory by scholars from the developing countries of South America[1]. Andre Gunder Frank led the charge against modernization, and in its stead, proposed the dependency theory as the vehicle to explain the development problems of Latin American and developing countries; as well to develop a model for the development processes of those countries. Andre Frank argued that the world's capitalist system has only led to development in some areas and the development of underdevelopment in others[2]. Paul Baran, through his book, *The political Economy of Growth*, is, however, credited with been instrumental to initiating the mindset that spurred the dependency movement.

Paul Baran had argued that it is in the interest of capitalism to keep the Third world backward as indispensable entities that provide the West with raw materials and opportunities to build economic surpluses[3]. He argued that with the exception of such colonies as Australia, New Zealand, and North America where immigrant Europeans held sway, the colonizers were determined to extract the largest possible gains from the colonies, and take the loot home[4]. The crux of Paul Baran's argument was that the development of the West countries then meant the underdevelopment of the underdeveloped countries.

Walter Rodney (1974-1980) also shared this belief as he argued in the book, *How Europe Underdeveloped Africa* that the advent of colonialism interrupted the natural course of development that was already in progress[5]. Walter Rodney insisted that colonialism shifted developmental emphasis away from the established forms of government, industry, and services to the forms of economic practices and situations that served the interests of the colonialists[6]. This colonialism destroyed the growth of indigenous technology such as the works of the indigenous goldsmiths, carpenters, architects, and artisans[7]. These mindsets gave rise to the dependency theory.

The dependency model segments nations into the core and the peripheral. The core nations are the wealthy nations that became developed by predating and dominating the periphery nations whose main role was to provide cheap labor and raw materials to the core. The benefits of this relationship accrue only to the core nations, which hence, grow richer and more developed to the detriment of the peripheral nations, from which, the core nations continually drain away their resources; and thus making them less developed. These dependency theorists, therefore, postulate that the products of history, domestic, and global institutions have played roles in reproducing these global inequalities that exists among nations[8].

Whereas the modernization model attributes the disparities in development to differences in the internal conditions within countries, the dependency model attributes the disparities to the initial relationships created among nations. The main thrusts of the dependency model are that the obstacles to the development of the underdeveloped economies are external; with the periphery countries been deprived of their surpluses.

Fernando Cardoso and Enzo Faletto, had, in *Dependency and Development in Latin America*, viewed the dependency model from the perspective of creating the pathway out of the periphery[9]. They argued that country's mode of historical insertion into the global market, which determines it degree of economic diversification, also defines its prospects for development[10]. Hence, countries that entered the global market primarily as suppliers of raw materials have obviously found it difficult to diversify[11].

Fernando Cardoso and Enzo Faletto also projected the perspective that, in the global economic system as was then constituted; development in the developed economies (core) essentially meant the underdevelopment of the underdeveloped economies (periphery). The underdeveloped nations would, therefore, have to break relationships with developed countries and pursue internal development and growth[12]; as the pathway out of the periphery[13].

Opponents have criticized the classical dependency model, suggesting some arbitrariness in the elimination of the possibility of the development for the developing countries arising from external relationships[14]. Another criticism was that the model failed to clearly define dependency; and that the political and economic mechanism for the conceptual articulation of the theory was poor[15]. Yet another criticism was that the linkages between the international economies, the national parameters for participating in the global economy, and the individual were not made[16].

Opponents have also contended that the rise of the East Asia countries to greater economic heights necessitates the rejection of the dependency theory as a useful tool for understanding the issues of industrialization of developing countries[17]. These opponents argued that for the same fact that several developing countries have, in varying degrees, succeeded in their industrialization through external relationships, the divide into North-South and core-periphery is diminishing in importance[18]. It does seem, however, that the successes of the Asian countries resulted from the restructuring of the global production system and the dispersal of manufacturing capacity to these developing Asian countries; thereby enabling the countries to industrialize[19].

Although the relevance of the dependency model may have diminished, the rapid economic development of such former peripheral countries as China, India, Brazil, and the East Asian Countries has made the singular perspective of global economic system more complex[20]. The prevailing perspective is that except for the East Asia countries, such other countries as China, Brazil and India seemed to have followed the dependency model on the need for re-organizing their internal dynamics for development rather than relational dependency on the core countries.

Obviously, the product of history, domestic and global institutions have played crucial roles in reproducing the inequalities that currently exist among nations; such domestic issues as quality of internal political institutions and leadership also play decisive roles. Under certain situations, therefore, the state could become proactive agents of development. As the rapid economic development of India, Brazil, and the some East Asian countries have shown, the adoption of democratic systems that combine openness to international market, social justice, and political accountability should be the development strategy for the developing countries.

Some scholars also do not accept that the importance of the dependency model is now totally diminished as the developing countries are still technologically dependent on the developed countries[21]. The periphery countries can, thus, be said to have progressively experienced three forms of dependency; colonial dependency, financial -industrial dependency, and technological-industrial dependency[22]. The technology-industrial dependency is, therefore, the new dependency[23]. This peripheral dependency has, therefore, not been static; but has rather been dynamic[24].

If the effects of dependency are extrapolated through the decades, Nigeria can be said to have progressively experienced the three forms of dependency; colonial dependency, financial - industrial dependency, and technological-industrial dependency. Unfortunately, the technology-industrial dependency is still the major impediment to national development in Nigeria. This is all the more crucial as the creation and communication of knowledge have become the new tools for wealth and job creation as the information technology (IT) industry has become a key for the development of a knowledge-based economy[25]. Obviously, the knowledge and technological gaps that still exist between the developed and developing countries, means that the dependency model is still potent.

Chapter 6

Lewis (Dual sector) model

William Arthur Lewis, the 1979 Nobel Prize winner in economics, articulated the dual sector model in a classic article, *Economic Development with Unlimited Supplies of Labor;* in which he also laid the foundation of developmental economics[1]. The basis of the Lewis theory of development is the postulation that surplus labor from traditional agricultural sectors is transferred to the modern industrial sector. This is, therefore, a development process triggered by the transfer of surplus labor from the traditional agrarian sector, in which the supply of labor is unlimited and workers are paid subsistence wages; to the new modern sector[2]. The dual sector model of development posits that the characters of the traditional agricultural sector are low wages, abundance of labor, and low productivity. The modern industrial sector on the other hand, offers higher wages, higher marginal productivity, and initial higher demand for more workers.

Over the time, the growth of the industrial sector absorbs the surplus labor; thereby promoting industrialization and stimulating sustainable development. As the surplus labor is been used, labor becomes scarcer, and workers are paid on the basis of their marginal product[3]. This transition from traditional to modern economic stage would, however, involve changes in attitudes, changes in the social and political institutions; as well as the creation of the needs for personal achievements[4].

This model presupposes that the traditional and modern societies are two different stages of development, with their differences disappearing as time progressed[5]. The model also projects a pathway toward development as well as industrialization that is financed by foreign capital[6]. Just like the modernization model, the underpinning assumption is that more investment leads to more growth and ultimately results in development[7]. This Lewis model is essentially the application of the Harrod-Domar in the context of less developed countries[8].

As modernization is also, essentially a development process that has been triggered by the transfer of surplus labor from the traditional agrarian sector to the new modern sector; it is hence, the extended end of the Lewis model[9]. The Lewis model of development is, however, more appropriate for the analysis of the development of rural communities.

Williams Arthur Lewis had also described the goal of economic development as that of closing the gap in income per capita between the rich and poor countries[10]. Unfortunately, the primary characteristics of such developing countries as Nigeria include low income per capita[11]. The argument can therefore be made that, although, growth cannot be equated to development, it has become one of the preconditions for meeting such development goals as poverty reduction.

Lewis was obviously more interested in the transition of developing economies from dualistic to the one sector of modern economic growth[12]. The proponents of the Lewis model indicate that the solution to the global development problems facing third world countries is to focus efforts toward changing the operational rules of the global economic system; as well as the acceptance of the power of technology in changing the two sectors[13]. The model is, however, criticized for the erroneous assumption that there is no cash capital accumulation in agriculture and that investments go only to non-agriculture sector[14]. Another criticism is that such a development model that is based on dual economy sets up inequality between the modern and traditional sectors[15]. Yet another criticism is that, with the presupposition that the traditional and modern societies are two different stages of development, segments of the society attract different policy attentions; thereby exacerbating the inequalities[16]. For that, critics argue that unless the inequality inherent in this duality of rural traditional segments of the society versus the modern urban segments is reduced through political or institutional means, there is the possibility that violence and political instability could derail the processes of development[17]. Obviously, the Lewis model, which accepts the power of technology in changing the two sectors, is still relevant in such heavily populated countries as China, India, Bangladesh, Central America and Sub-Saharan African countries like Nigeria[18].

Chapter 7

Analyzing the other Development Models

Although the modernization model, the dependency model, and the Lewis model are the most canvassed models of development, the Rostovian model, the Harrod-Domar model, the world system, and the state theory model, are nonetheless not less contentious.

Rostovian Model

Former MIT scholar and Director of Policy and planning in the State department of the United States, Walter Rostow, an ardent advocate of development through the pathway of modernization postulated this development model in a 1960 book, *The Stages of Economic Growth: A Non-Communist Manifesto.* The Rostovian model posits that economic development occurs in five stages of transition from the traditional society; creating the preconditions for take-off; take-off; drive to maturity; and high mass consumption. The first stage is characterized by agriculture and low productivity. The introduction of trade and its attendant increase in investments constitute the second (pre-conditions for take-off) stage. At the third stage, economic growth becomes a permanent feature; whereas the fourth stage entails that every aspect of the economy has become modernized, and capable of absorbing new technologies. The fifth and final stage is when the economy has expanded beyond the level of meeting only basic needs.

This model symbolizes a "take-off" to "self-sustained growth" perspective[1]. The Rostovian model is essentially the presentation of modernization from the perspective of developmental economics[2]. Countries go through "stages of growth" as leaders seek to transform their traditional and agrarian societies into industrial economies[3]. The industrialized nations have gone through the first three stages and are now "self-sustaining growths"[4]. The developing countries should follow the same to propel themselves into sustainable growth[5].

Harrod-Domar Model

An underlying assumption of the Harrod-Domar model is that an increase in output would provide the basis for further growth because of the reinvestment of part of the output[6]. Capital accumulation is of relative importance in this model[7]. As incomes become higher, the propensity to save increases; reinvestment also increases; thereby fueling more economic growth. Once this process commences, it becomes self-sustaining[8].

This model postulates that the problem of underdeveloped countries is their inability to remove the fetters that prevent development. The Harrod-Domar model is essentially an economic growth model rather than an economic development model[9].

World system Model

The world system model is largely associated with the sociologist Immanuel Wallerstein in his 1974 work, *The Modern World System: Capitalist Agriculture and the Origins on the European World-Economy in the Sixteen Century*. The world system theorists postulate that the 'world-system' and not the nation states is the primary mover of development[10]. The world-system model portrays the state as a group of elites that serve their self-interests[11]. The traces of the world system theory, which had emerged in the 1970s and 1980s, had criticized the emphasis of the modernization model on the state as the only economic unit; and its assumption that there is only a single pathway to development of all nations. The modernization model was also criticized for its utter disregard of the historical and local constraint to the development of some nations.

Like the dependency model, the world system model segments the modern world-system into core, and periphery nations; but goes to add another segment, the semi-periphery nations. The postulation is that as the core exploits the semi-periphery; and the semi-periphery in turn, exploits the periphery. The world system model positions the modern economic system as that in which the core countries focus on dominating higher skills and capital intensive production; whereas, the peripheral and semi-peripheral countries are respectively confined to low-skill and labor-intensive production; and extraction of raw materials[12].

Considering that the world system model is also based on the core-periphery segmentation, it is an obvious follow-up to the dependency theory[13]. Like the dependency theory it also sought to focus on the critical perspectives of the inequalities that exist among nations[14]. This model, however, holds the state system model in distrust.

State System Model

Contrary to the postulations of the world system model, the perspective of the state system model is that development involves interactions between the state and social institutions; and that the nature of such relationships affects the developmental capabilities of the state. Development, therefore, depends on the internal and external stability; as well as the influence of the state. The take-off in the development process of each state is unique to that country. The function of the state in a capitalist system is, therefore, to create the conditions in which capital accumulations create social harmony; and the state uses its monopoly over legitimate use of force to impose social order[15]. The state is therefore required to take control of the developmental processes. As Fernando Cardoso and Enzo Faletto had also argued in the book, *Dependency and Development in Latin America*, under certain situations, the state could become proactive agents of development[16]. Although, the world system model holds the state system model in distrust; the inequalities, inherent in state systems, could be reversed through social democratic and labor movements that arise from the world-system[17].

The Japanese developmental model has created some measure of ambiguity in the interpretation of the development theories. Although pro-western scholars considered the post-war II modernization of Japan as a vindication of the western model, others saw is as an adaptation of the western model to the unique Japanese values and culture. The Japanese model has thus been portrayed as different; characterized by high saving rates, educated workforce, outward-looking policies and institutional enhancement[18]. The success of Japan apparently arose from the combination of their cultural orientation toward high saving rates (Harrod-Domar model), outward-looking orientation (modernization model), and institutional enhancement (state system model).

Chapter 8

Conceptualizing Comparative Advantages

The comparative advantage theories are contingent on the concepts that trade could be used as basis for development. David Ricardo's theory of comparative advantage indicates that countries could benefit from international trade by exporting those products in which they have the greatest comparative advantage. This principle postulates that a country would export those goods and services in which it has low opportunity costs and import those in which it has higher opportunity costs[1]. By specializing in the products and services in which they have comparative advantages, the aggregate production output would increase. This theory finds support from some scholars who indicate that trade across borders is an extension of the process of specialization that lies at the heart of economic growth; with mutual benefits arising as each trading partner specializes wherever their comparative advantage lies[2].

Essentially, the theory canvasses that a country's relative factor scarcity determines its comparative advantage[3]. By this, a country will export the goods and services that use its abundant factors with more intensity if there are no impediments to international trade[4]. The underlying but erroneous assumption of this theory is that, when considering two countries involved in trade; (i) each produces two different goods using labor as the only factor of production; (ii) labor is identical within but not across countries, (iii) there is full employment of labor and (iv) no transportation costs[5]. These assumptions are obviously not realistic; thereby creating distortions in the global markets. The David Ricardo theory of comparative advantage is, therefore, essential to trade because, by countries specializing in the products and services in which they have comparative advantages, the aggregate production output would increase.

The Heckscher-Ohlin model of comparative advantage is an extension of the Ricardo's model; but instead of a single factor of production (labor), the model has two of the labor, land, capital, and natural resources[6]. The Heckscher-Ohlin (H-O) theory of factor endowment indicates that the international and interregional differences in production costs arise out of the differences in supply of production factors.

The comparative advantage and the Heckscher-Ohlin models are traditional trade theories that emphasize static comparative advantages as basis of international trade[7]. In these traditional trade theories, a country's factor endowment is downplayed and technologies treated as given. Also the market is assumed as perfect and adjustments to shocks are assumed as instantaneous and without costs.

This is not the situation is real life and hence, the dynamic theories recognize the existence of the involving and less instantaneous adjustment processes of the static trade theories. A dynamic comparative advantage and the resulting competitiveness in international trade involve a process of constant searching and learning, under conditions of uncertainty[8]. This enhances a country's production capacities and trades; enhanced by how much it lends itself to the processes of learning and searching.

The concept of comparative advantage indicates that whereas such factors as abundance of cheap labor gives such Sub-Saharan Africa as Nigeria a comparative advantage on the supplies of raw materials; technological advantages give the developed countries the comparative advantages over the production of machinery and equipment. The implication of the theory of comparative advantage would be that less developed countries should not embark on industrialization; but rather, the basis of their comparative advantage should lie on the primary production of goods[9].

Likewise, the Heckscher-Ohlin theory expects such countries as Nigeria that have abundance of raw materials and labor to concentrate on the labor-intensive raw material production whereas the advanced countries, with abundance of capital and technical know-how to concentrate on the capital-intensive equipment and machinery. Even when the theory of dynamic comparative advantage is applied, the developed countries, by virtue of their technological advancement still have the dynamic comparative advantage over such Sub-Saharan African countries as Nigeria.

Obviously, the factors that enhance the economic growth of

a country would include the improvement in productivity, increasing export potentialities, and the attraction of foreign investments. However, to create the export potentialities, a country's export product would need to be competitive in foreign markets. Often, the opportunity cost of the production of a product defines a country's comparative advantages on the product.

Chapter 9

Conceptualizing Globalization

Globalization emphasizes the interrelationship among countries as well as the changes and development in global issues[1]. Globalization rests on the premise that it would enhance global competition by allowing countries concentrate on those goods and services in which they have competitive edges. From an economic perspective, globalization is the integration of economies around the world trades and financial transactions. By describing modernization as a historical process by which agrarian societies transit into industrialized societies, globalization could be considered as a part of the modernization process[2].

From the 1990s, globalization seemed to have taken over the position the modernization theory used to hold[3]. The main instrument of globalization is the World Trade organization. According to the 1994 Marrakesh agreement that laid its fundamental principles, the World Trade Organization (WTO) was set up essentially to achieve a substantial reduction of tariffs and barriers to trade[4].

Globalization has also been described as an economic

phenomenon entailing the interdependence of national economies in trade, finance and macroeconomic policy[5]. Some of its objectives include raising the standards of living and volume of real income. The globalization process, however, has had more to do with increased technological innovation and information flows than foreign trade and investment per se[6].

This concept has, however, been very contentious. Proponents argue that the free and unhindered trade is obviously better than trade with restrictions because it improves competition in the domestic market, thereby giving consumers better quality products and services. Free trade also expands the market; creating the opportunities for the producers and investors from other markets.

Whereas most developed countries project the concept as essential to global development and trade, the developing countries have argued that globalization runs against their economic interest. Even in those areas in which the countries had comparative advantages (like in cash cropping), biogenetic processes have turned the competitive edges to the more developed economies.

Opponents argue that globalization and free trades benefit the corporations and capitalists while hurting the global environment, local cultures, and the workers. Economic groups (like council on Economic priorities) blame globalization for widespread child labor, terrible working conditions, and mass poverty in the poor countries because international competition drives firms to pressure the governments for weaker regulation[7].

Moreover, under the rules regarding the globalization of trades and investment, business organizations have an incentive to move their highly polluting activities to nations that have the least rigorous environment regulations[8]. In such countries, even such taken-for-granted issues as good standard of living wages, workplace safety, environmental protection, and prohibition of child labor that form the bedrock of ethical corporate practices in the developed countries are rarely canvassed when the same companies operate in developing countries Globalization has in fact, expanded worldwide profit-making opportunities that border on predatory behavior[9].

With regards to such Sub-Saharan countries as Nigeria, proponents argue that globalization has given them access to the international market by making it possible for these countries to achieve efficiency in the use of their factor endowments. This also increases the country's revenues and improves the balance of trade by selling her products to international market. The proponents also argue that globalization has led to the improvement in living standards and life expectancy within these countries. By opening an economy, the country can trade with other countries through economic integration. A major additional factor from national gains from trade is the increase in varieties of products that become available to consumers through imports as countries open to trade. Globalization has, however, also produced uneven results across nations and people.

In contrast, opponents argue that globalization has only brought much benefit to the developed world and has virtually brought none to most of the developing countries, including Nigeria. They argue that World trade agreements did not adequately take cognizance of the peculiarities of the developing countries; but was rather a case of one-suits-all. The unfortunate situation is that most developing countries do not have enough developmental edges in expertise and capital resources to be competitive.

These situations exist even in the areas in which they hitherto had comparative advantages like cash crop production as biogenetic processes in crop production have turned over the competitive edge to more developed economies. More so, the cheaper imports arising from globalization are gradually destroying the fragile local industries in the developing countries. Hence, a key issue with free trade is the tendency to inhibit the growth of infant local industries that need protection from the multi-national corporations that have already attained higher levels of efficiency.

The concept of the free trade component of globalization also requires that countries remove or reduce the tariffs on imports. The developing countries cannot, however, really reduce tariffs if they are to protect their infant industry and prevent product dumping into their economies. Infant industries are burdened with very high start-up costs that may require some protection if such industries would survive. Hence, trade restrictions are used to nurture such industries in their infancy because most developing countries do not have the required developmental expertise and capital resources to be competitive. These are, therefore, some of the reasons for the governments of the developing countries to impose tariffs on the importation of certain goods.

In addition, the purported globalization benefits of possible transfer of technological and management skills have not been the case in most developing countries. The biggest losers continue to be the developing (and underdeveloped) economies because the cheaper imports arising from globalization are gradually destroying the fragile local industries in the developing countries. This in turn, is creating job dislocation and displacement; which in turn, could create social and political instabilities.

Globalization benefits the few developed countries and hurts the majority that constitutes the developing economies as it has failed to yield benefits; as the share of the population living in poverty has continued to rise[10]. It does seem that globalization has and would only continue to widen the real income gap between African countries and the developed world and may eventually undermine the powers of African nation-states by creating political and social instabilities. Globalization has essentially further fostered the exploitation of African economies; thereby widening the income gap between African countries and the rest of the world[11].

Obviously, the linkages between the international economy, the national parameters for participating in the global economy and the individual have not been made[12]. Under globalization, most Sub-Saharan African countries have apparently become compelled to been a part of this zero-sum game in which economic goals can only at the cost of sacrificing political and social goals[13]. The challenge is on grappling with how to efficiently deploy the functions of adjusting the capital markets without paying for the social price of unequal distribution that usually betrays the values of true democratic societies[14].

Chapter 10

Democracy and Development

The predominant findings from quantitative comparative researches show positive correlations between socio-economic development and democracy[1]. The reasons for the positive relationship of democracy and development are principally because economic development spreads authority and democratic aspirations among variety or people, thereby fostering democracy[2]. The primary determinants of the likelihood of democratic transition are; income per capita, the distribution of wealth and educational levels[3]. The thrust of this postulation is that democracy is most likely when levels of development are not low, income inequalities are not high and the citizens are not poorly educated.

The modernization theory assumes that the development process is an accumulation of social changes that readies and culminates to the democratization of a nation[4]. The modernization theorists also emphasize theories of democratic pluralism; a political approach which projects structural functionalism that assumes that despite structural difference, all political systems perform similar functions[5]. This concept presents a value neutral framework for comparing political systems irrespective of the culture and history of the society[6].

The increased levels of economic development are associated with democracy[7]. Similarly, economic development can actually engineer democracy[8]. These perspectives both fall within the broader modernization theory that assumes that there is a universal process of socio-economic development of which democracy is not the final stage[9].

Some researchers have found positive relationships between democratic governance and such human development indicators as education[10] and public services[11]. Democracies promote human capital development through investments in healthcare and education, thus contributing to economic growth[12]. Economic development substantially improves a nation's democratic prospects[13]. The modernization theory also postulates that development or modernization will lead to democracy[14].

Obviously, positive linear relationships exist between the levels of development and democratic development[15]. This is because, economic development, which, involves industrialization, high educational standards, and steady increase in the overall wealth of the society is a basic condition sustaining democracy[16]. Socioeconomic development is, therefore, a necessary condition for the sustenance of a democratic system[17]. When, hence, performance is measured in terms of public services, genuine democratic governments clearly outperform authoritarian regimes because they reduce opportunities for rent-seeking behavior[18]. The stability of the democratic system is, however, dependent on the effectiveness and legitimacy of the political system[19].

Although, most scholars generally agree on a linkage between development and democracy; the disagreements hinge on the causal direction of the relationship as well as the level of development. Some scholars, have hence, challenged the suggested linear relationship between economic development and democracy, especially for the developed countries[20]. Some scholars indicate that development and democracy are largely independent processes; insisting that there is no direct relationship between economic growth and transition or consolidation of democracy[21]. The assessments of these scholars are not wholesome enough as they equate democracy with the mere conduct of elections. When democracy accurately reflects the will of the electorates, over the time, it usually leads to economic development.

The earlier proponents of the modernization model had sought to tie the persistent coincidence of democratic political system and development to the application of the theory. Hence, the assumption always has been that development is inherently beneficial to societies and should be promoted through the removal of the various obstacles to development. Using these political perspectives of the modernization theory, the key to political development is, however, an electorate that is both willing and able to participate in domestic politics[22]

Although, a country's mode of historical insertion into the global market, determines it degree of economic diversification and defining its prospects for development; such domestic issues as quality of internal political institutions also play decisive roles. There seems to be a persistent coincidence of democratic political system and national development. The external investors are not likely to invest in countries that fail to meet the threshold of effective governance in regulatory and legal systems that guarantee freedom of transactions, property rights, and transparency of government processes. The democratic systems that combine openness to international market, social justice and political accountability should, therefore, be the development strategy for the developing countries. Creating and sustaining genuine practices of the democratic system; as well as combining openness to international market, social justice, and political accountability should also be a development strategy for Nigeria[23].

PATH III

Development and its Indicators

Chapter 11

Development and its Indicators

Development is when a group of human species in a geographical location, acquires the capacities to understand natural laws that enable them to collectively organize to increase their capacity of production through technological innovations[1]. Development occurs when a society or any human unit acquires the social, economic, political and technological wherewithal to understand the laws of nature and its environment, and uses that to attain the capacities that enable it meet the needs of its citizens[2]. Some studies have defined the concept of development in terms of economic performance, operationalizing it with real GDP per capita or energy consumption.

Traditionally, development was equated with the growth of income per capita. Starting from the 1970s, however, other indicators of development have emerged through the works of development economists[3]. They contended that development is more comprehensive than economic growth; and that essentially, the latter is a part of the former[4]. Such concepts as the provision of basic needs, creation of employment, and achievement of more equitable income distribution have, therefore, become criteria for evaluating the level of development that exists in a country[5].

Accordingly, the United Nations Development Program (UNDP) elevated educational attainment, health standards to income per capita as the main indicators of development[6]. The human development index (HDI) of countries have been adopted as the summary index that measures a country's average achievements in three basic aspects of human development-health, knowledge and a decent standard of living[7]. Health is measured by life expectancy at birth, knowledge by a combination adult literacy and gross school enrollment ratio, and standard of living by GDP per capita in the US dollar-based purchasing power parity[8].

Educational attainment component comprises of adult literacy rates, and the combined gross enrollment ratio for primary, secondary and tertiary schools, weighted to give adult literacy more significance in the statistics[9]. The education index thus measures from 0-1, with 1.0 as the highest level. A literacy rate of 75% rates as 0.75. The education index for Nigeria has consistently averaged at a low score of .44.

The health index is calculated using a minimum value for the expectancy of 25 years and maximum of 85 years; and measures the relative achievement of a country in life expectancy at birth and ranges from 0-1. A health index of 55% rates as 0.5. Nigeria's health index has ranged within the low scores of .40 and .50.

The standard of living is measured by gross domestic product per capita. This Gross Domestic Product, which been adjusted for purchasing power parity (PPP), is used to determine the GDP index that measures the GDP per capita, adjusted for the US dollar-based purchasing power parity. For Nigeria, this index has remained between abysmally low values of 0.37 to 0.43. Nigeria is, therefore, a low development nation; comparing with Ghana (0.56), Botswana (0.63), and South Africa (0.63) as medium development nations, and Mauritius (0.74) as a high development nation.

Chapter 12

Internal factors constraining development in Nigeria

A country's mode of historical insertion into the global market, which determines it degree of economic diversification; could also define its prospects for development unless effective policy measures are adopted to remove the internal factors constraining the development. Although countries that entered the global market primarily as suppliers of raw materials have obviously found it difficult to diversify, public policies could be used to effect the necessary changes needed to usher in national development. Those factors that enhance the economic growth of a country, namely; improvement in productivity, increasing export potentialities, and the attraction of foreign investments, would also enhance its overall development.

Although, each country has its own unique development problems that are contingent on both internal and external factors; such domestic issues as quality of internal political institutions and leadership play crucial and decisive roles. Economic factors, adverse world market, and non-participation in the global supply chain can, therefore, no longer adequately explain the poor developmental performance of Nigeria. Nigeria is in need of a "social democracy" that combines openness to international market, social justice and political accountability as the development strategy; that is also hinged on the pursuit of inward looking investment and trade policies.

The internal factors that constrain development in Nigeria include; the internalization of the effects of colonization, nature of governance, political conflicts, the adverse effects of corruption, and the lack of a well-defined private property system.

Internalization of Historical Factors

The continuous internalization of the experiences of colonization is still an issue in the underdevelopment of Nigeria[1]. There are obvious distinctions between the experiences of such former 'colonies of settlement' (as the United States, Australia, and Argentina) and the sub-Saharan African 'colonies of exploitation' as Nigeria[2]. The negative spill-overs of colonization have created the tendency of most African nations to be skeptical about foreign investors; which adversely affects FDI inflows to the region[3].

Nature of Governance

A state in which corruption and "neopatrimonialism" are prevalent would always suffer in relations to modernization. Personalized political authorities characterize the neopatrimonial state; weak checks on the private appropriation of public resources and excessive "clientism" are other characteristics[4]. The weak institutions and political insecurity, centralization and arbitrary exercise of power have also been associated with neopatrimonial governance[5].

In Nigeria, the neopatrimonial nature of governance shares a chunk of the blame for the failures of the states as the agents of development[6]. In most of the federating states of the nation, political opportunism rather than developmental objectives tend to drive policymaking[7]. The protruding situation becomes that social and economic advancement become dependent on one's relationship to political power rather than the effective use of economic resources.

More so, the personalized distributions of state resources are leveraged over the welfare-enhancing public goods and services[8]. This neopatrimonial nature of governance, coupled with the weakness of state institutions in checking private appropriation of public resources fuel bureaucratic corruption, thereby reducing the effectiveness of public service, as well as national development.

Effects of corruption

Another constraint to the development of the Nigeria is the prevalence of political and bureaucratic corruption. Corruption is not only detrimental to the society; but also to business as well[9]. Corruption leads to misallocation of resources, disrupts economic development, and distorts public policies[10]. The International Monetary Fund (IMF) had determined that countries with high corruption levels have less of their GPD going into investment[11].

The World Bank also identifies corruption as the greatest obstacle to economic and social development because it distorts the rule of law and weakening the foundations of public institutions[12]. Corruption slows down economic development, crowds out productive investment, raises the cost of business, and reduces the products and public projects[13]. These vices are capable of repressing economic development and productivity. Moreover, money and resources are likely to flow out to other countries in which the investment climates are more favorable. Obviously, such vices slow down the process of modernization.

The issues of political and bureaucratic corruption must come to fore when considerations are made on the political and governance issues that besiege Nigeria; and must be confronted if the aims of the so-called millennium development goals are to be realized.

Political Conflicts

For the state to develop, a focus on internal and external stability is an imperative. Unfortunately, political instability and ethnic conflicts have remained prominent parts of the political and social landscapes of Nigeria.

Obviously, ethnic inequality destroys political stability. Hence, countries that have invested in those policies and institutions that have increased their ability to manage and reduce social tensions have experienced lower levels of political instability[14].

Although ethnic fragmentation in Nigeria is responsible for a significant part of its political instability and corruption; it must be noted that it is the stability or instability of the political process that could promote or wreck the growth prospects of the country.

Lack of Well-defined Property rights Systems

The main basis of development in the western world seems to be a well-developed property rights system. Economic specialization, which is the main ingredient of modernization, requires well-defined property rights[15]. The property rights systems of nations are, however, shaped by historical and socio-economic conditions within such countries[16]. Unfortunately, the characteristics that the third world countries like Nigeria have in common is a very underdeveloped property rights system and weak legal apparatuses to create, protect, and enforce these right to an extent as to create sustainable development[17]. In the underdeveloped countries, the majority does not have property rights, cannot enter into long term contracts; and cannot, therefore, obtain credits[18].

Ultimately, the task would be to create a legal and market system that would benefit all and sundry. Nigeria must, therefore, develop well-defined property rights systems that place legal and well-defined ownerships on such tangible assets as land, automobiles, and market stalls, mortgages. This should not, however, be about copying the statute books of the western world; but rather about designing and implementing property laws in alignment with the cultural orientation of the country.

PATH IV

The Pathways to Development

Chapter 13

The Modernization Model: A pathway to Development

Modernization is the historic process by which agrarian societies transit into industrialized societies[1]. The concept of modernization could also be seen as a process in which underdeveloped countries catch up with the developed countries; but not only in the context of the economy but also in relations to technology[2]. The essence of modernization is not only industrialization, but also of changes in attitudes, social values, and lifestyles[3].

The earlier proponents of modernization had suggested the industrialized Western countries as the prototypes for modernization, and had sought to tie the persistent coincidence of democratic political system and development to the application of the theory [4]. Hence, in one of his pioneering works, titled, *The Stages of Political Development,* Abrano Fimo Kenneth Organski, indicated that the modernization theory is in consonance with democratic pluralism. The earlier modernization concepts were, therefore, hinged on western concept of development[5].

Development is inherently beneficial to societies and must be promoted through the removal of the various obstacles to development[6]. One conceptualization of the modernization theory, therefore, is the belief that underdeveloped countries must follow the social and political practices of the developed countries to attain the levels of human development comparable to those of the developed countries.

The Rostovian model had expanded the economic perspective of the modernization theory into stages of economic growth; outlining development as five progressive stages of economic growth, namely from traditional society, pre-conditions for take-off, take-off, road to maturity and age of high mass consumption. As the Rostovian model outlined, countries go through "stages of growth" as leaders seek to transform their traditional and agrarian societies into industrial economies; industrialized nations have gone through the first three stages and are now "self-sustaining growths"; and the developing countries should, therefore, follow the same to propel themselves into sustainable growth[7].

The relationship between modernization and national development emanates from different perspectives as modernization has been widely accepted as the process of transforming social, economic, and political system into their modern states[8]. From the political perspective, the modernized governmental system must exhibit high levels of differentiation and functional specialization in governance; adopting rational decision-making procedures. Also, political activities should be hinged on law, becoming more open, and hence increasing democratic consciousness[9]. The key to political development is an electorate that is both willing and able to participate in domestic politics[10]. Thus, political participation plays a crucial role in economic development[11]. Strong democratic political culture can be highly supportive of efforts to address development problems; thereby establishing the basis for sustained economic growth[12].

In terms of social structures, the modernized societies are stratified; with roles and social status defined by personal abilities and achievements[13]. Public service assumes a bureaucratic posture and the function and status of the family diminishes[14]. Culturally, modern societies become more formalized and programmed; making cultural activities clearer to the extent that cultural diversities become increasingly obscured. On individual levels, motivation for success is higher, and initiatives and creativity become more relevant.

From the economic perspective, the manufacturing and service sectors are leveraged over other sectors, with more reliance on inanimate than animate. In addition, manufacturing hinges on the continuous and mass production of standardized products [15]. Education is the key to the development of the modern society[16]. The advancement of science and technology also plays a key role; and when introduced to less developed countries, triggers economic growth and development[17].

Essentially, the modernization theory conceptualizes development as a movement along a continuum of historical changes all nations follow[18]. This continuum is that path of societal evolution that was followed by the developed nations and should ultimately be traveled by the underdeveloped countries[19]. The indices of modernization include gross national product, income per capita, and acceptance of universally defined "modern" values, social differentiation, and political integration.

As indicated earlier, the modernization model has experienced some infusion of ideas from scholars and development economists from the developing countries as they challenge previous assumption that the western pattern of development is the only path to modernization; arguing instead, that there are different pathways to modernization. Unlike the Western theorists, these new theorists acknowledge the significance of the external environment on the processes of modernization.

Instead of presuming that tradition and modernity are at opposite ends, the new theorists believe both can coexist and supplement each other[20]. Instead of seeing tradition as an obstacle to the drive toward modernization, the new theorists argue that some traditional elements are capable of exerting positive effects on the drive toward modernization. Immanuel Wallerstein, therefore, recommended three development strategies for the developing countries; (i) the strategy of seizing the chance through aggressively transforming state structures of comparative advantages actions, using the instruments of the state, (ii) promoting development based on existing comparative advantages, and (ii) self-reliance through inward orientation and integration[21].

Chapter 14

Genuine Electoral Competition: A force for Development

A positive correlation exists between the level of human development and the level of electoral competition in a democratic nation[1]. The reasons for the positive relationship of genuine electoral competition and human development are that the educational empowerment spreads political awareness among the citizens; which, thereby, further fosters democratic ideals[2]. Elections are genuine when they are competitive; the will of the voters freely expressed; and votes are counted honestly and accurately.

Electoral competition creates a balance between the politician who is supposed to supply good governance and the citizens who demand good governance[3]. Electoral competition also creates and guarantees accountability, imposes constraints on executive arbitrariness, and improves representation, and participation.

Studies have predominantly shown that electoral competition brings improvement in leadership by incentivizing leaders to deliver on public goods and services. Obviously, under the democratic system, voters are expected to reward good leadership and punish poor performances. Although, these voters have limited means for checking the behavior of elected leaders, elections generally allow them to re-elect or throw out the incumbent representatives and officials. This ability to re-elect or throw out elected official does not depend exclusively on the real, anticipated or perceived performance of the incumbent but also on the anticipated performance of the opposition[4].

Arising from the concerns of the elected official on this possibility of losing voters' support to the opposition, electoral competition makes the political leadership to be more responsive and more accountable[5]. The tendency to convert public resources is discouraged; and the welfare-enhancing public goods are encouraged when governments are pressured to be responsive and accountable.

Electoral competition, therefore, offers the advantage of rooting public policies in political accountability[6]. Moreover, by encouraging public accountability, electoral competition imposes checks on the leadership[7]. In ideal democratic settings, when incumbent governments sense that the opposition is strong and credible enough to take power, they act in ways that would enhance public satisfaction with their activities[8]. Electoral competition fosters responsiveness and accountability, improves quality of governance, enhances political stability, induces human rights protection, encourages credible opposition, and fosters human development.

The conduct of genuine electoral competition brings

improvement in leadership by incentivizing leaders to deliver on public goods and services; and, therefore, relates to improvements in such governance quality dimension as economic policy cohesion, public service effectiveness, and limited corruption. Thus, when performance is measured in terms of spending on welfare of the citizenry, genuine electoral competition improves governance[9]. There are, hence, positive effects of electoral competition on political leadership performance[10]. Obviously, some governance qualities, political, and policy incentives can only be canvassed through improvements in the quality of governance; which, in turn, can be improved through improvement in the level of electoral competition.

As genuine democracy and good governance go together, then electoral competition and political leadership performance will share positive relationships. Genuine electoral competition creates the good governance; and does not only contribute to transparency and accountability in government operations, but also creates sustainable economic environment for both the citizens and foreign investors; thereby enhancing national development.

The fundamental difference in disposition and performance among democratic regimes are reflections of the differences in quality of electoral competition. Obviously, the positive developmental outcomes of democracy in the Western world are largely due to the high level of democratic competition in those countries. To join the Western world in reaping the positive benefits of democratization, Nigeria and other so-called democratic states, will have to improve the level of electoral competition to the acceptable level.

Chapter 15

Foreign Direct Investment: A tool for Development

Although, development economists have always dealt with the contentious issue of whether or not foreign direct investment (FDI) is an agent of exploitation; it is apparent that it could also be a driving force for development[1]. Foreign Direct investment (FDI) could be the engine of economic growth; contributing to domestic investment, enhancing foreign technology absorptive capacity, assisting in technology transfers, and promoting international trade integration of the host country[2]. Scholars regard foreign direct investment as the measure of foreign ownership in such assets as; production factories, mines, land, and other tangible assets.

A rationale for pushing for FDI is on the basis that it engineers growth, and produces such externalities and technological transfers; as well as other spillovers as employment. FDI promotes growth by encouraging new technology and acquisition of new production and management skills[3]. FDI could, therefore, ease the transfer of technology and managerial knowledge; which can, in turn, spillover to the entire country[4]. FDI gives more resources, facilitates technology, and managerial transfers to host nations[5]. FDI thereby becomes a diffuser of technology, linking it to economic growth[6]. FDI provides capital for investment, provides employment, managerial skills and technology; thereby accelerating growth[7].

FDI has a significant positive effect on the economic growth of the host country; as it acts as a diffuser of technology; promotes growth by encouraging new technology, and encourages the acquisition of new production and management skills[8]. In most studies conducted on FDI inflows for a broad cross-section of countries, there were indications of positive roles in generating economic growth[9].

Although, the consensus is not total on the relationship between FDI and growth, there have been new theories that highlight the role of FDI in the improvement of technology and efficiency in the host countries[10]. Essentially, the expected contribution of FDI to growth is as a result of its role as a conduit for transfer of technology from the industrialized to the developing economies[11]. The positive impact of FDI is, however, only experienced when certain conditions prevail in the host country. The host country must be capable of absorbing the technology that spills over from the FDI[12].

Although various perspectives have been canvassed on the relationship of FDI to development of host countries, one potent view is that the positive relationships exist only when the host country has a minimum threshold of human capital; high with real income per capita, and has well-developed financial markets[13]. A second perspective is that the positive impact of FDI is experienced only when a country has a stock of human capital or a threshold of absorptive capacity[14].

Yet another perspective is a positive relationship exists when domestic and foreign capital complement each other; when the country achieves a certain threshold of development, when the country's education exceeds a certain threshold, when the country achieves a certain level of income and has a well-developed financial sector[15]. Essentially, for FDI to have a significant impact on growth, the host country must have attained a higher level of economic and human capital development. Obviously, the developed countries always benefit from technology spillovers from FDI because their human capital capacities have always exceeded the minimum threshold levels for the absorption of technology.

In most countries, the capital for development is derivable from domestic savings; loans from private and multilateral organizations; and from foreign direct investment. Most developed economies obtain the capital from all the mentioned sources. In most developing countries, however, access to capital is limited to aids from foreign donors and some measure of FDI. In recent years capital from donor countries and organizations have been dwindling, thereby increasing the need for FDI.

Compared with 40% for Asia and 12% for Latin America, the 48% poverty in Sub-Saharan Africa (SSA) is the highest in the world[16]. According to the Millennium Development Goal (MDG) an increase in FDI is capable of reducing the poverty rates (populations living under one dollar a day) in countries of SSA by half in the year 2015[17]. This situation is worst when broken down to country by country analysis. For instance the poverty rate is 62% for Burkina Faso, 66 % for Central African Republic, 73 % for Mali, 70 % for Nigeria and 64% for Zambia[18]. In its millennium declaration, the United Nations resolved to take special measures to increase the flow FDI as well as transfers of technologies to Africa[19].

The New partnership for African Development (NEPAD) declaration had stipulated that to meet its MDG, the Sub-Saharan African countries would need to fill a resource gap of $64 billion; which constitutes about 12% of its total GDP[20]. This resource gap has to come from either institutional loans, foreign aids, domestic savings or FDI.

In Nigeria, businesses do not access the international capital markets; income levels are low-hence little or no savings; foreign aids are dwindling; leaving FDI as a viable route to investment capital and as a potential tool for the alleviation of poverty. This need for foreign capital has become more important because the lack of foreign capital inflow could slow down the ability of the nation to pursue economic growth that is needed to create higher standard of living for its citizens[21]. Considering that most businesses in Nigeria do not also have access to the international capital market, FDIs as sources of capital becomes an imperative[22].

Obviously, the creation of a positive relationship between FDI and growth is dependent on the foreign investment policies adopted by the host country[23]. In pertinent terms, for instance,

FDI contributed to China's road to modernization through the path of industrialization by transforming an agrarian economy to an economy in which the tertiary sectors play central roles[24]. FDI still remains relevant to the economic growth of China today.

For reasons of history and cultural differences, however, the FDI-attracting public policies that worked in China may not work in Nigeria. Generally, these scholars agree that the exogenous components of FDI do not have significant influence on economic growth. It is the endogenous components that determine if or not FDI would create growth or not. In recent decades, some Sub-Sahara African countries have attracted more FDI due to proactive and investor-friendly policies[25]. To stimulate FDI therefore, Nigeria would need to improve its legal system, reduce bureaucratic bottlenecks, improve the country's infrastructure; as well as carry out some systemic reforms.

PATH V

Foreign Direct Investment:

Factors, Trends, and Constraints

Chapter 16

Primary Factors of Foreign Direct Investment

Increments in foreign investments can be used as one measure of economic growth and development. From this perspective of economic growth, there are vertical and horizontal perspectives to Foreign Direct Investment (FDI); both with different motives and determinants. The horizontal FDI is domestic market-oriented whereas the vertical FDI is export-oriented. Whereas the horizontal FDI is more likely to be affected by market potential, the vertical FDI would be affected by factor costs[1].

Often it is the nature of the FDI that determines the influencing factors. For instance, whereas the determinants for investments in service sector are likely to be availability of human capital; investments in manufacturing are influenced by good infrastructures[2]. Likewise, when organizations plan to invest in countries with infrastructure constraints or political instability, they go into joint ventures with local partners[3]. Other kinds of investment could, however, be in the form of subsidiaries, mergers, or share acquisition.

Investment decisions are driven fundamentally by the expected returns on investment and the assessed risks associated with the investments[4]. When considering investing abroad, therefore, multi-national organizations and institutionalized investors are always concerned about such issues as the political, economic and regulatory conditions that facilitate the understanding of the market size; repatriation of profits; risks of political instability; and the fiscal policies with the associated taxes.

Obviously, a new entrant has to understand the potential threats to market growth and the general business environment. There are, therefore, certain conditions that affect and influence the level of FDI in a country, namely; the country risk analysis, cost of production inputs, the legal framework, and the protection of intellectual property.

Country Risks analysis: Political and Economic Climates

Country risk, a summary of measure of economic and political stability has a strong influence on the flows of FDI[5]. Country risks are the broad range of actions taken or permitted by a country; which are capable of generating unfavorable consequences to foreign investors[6]. There exists an inverse relationship between political risks and the flow of FDI[7]. Political instability lowers economic growth by raising uncertainty and reducing the quality of the economic policy formulation[8]. The assessment of a country's risks is of fundamental importance to multinational organizations and financial institutions when they consider investing or extending loans and credit to foreign countries[9]. This assessment gives these organizations insight about the countries to invest or avoid.

The risks of investing abroad arise when there are political instabilities, unfavorable regulations on the particular industry, unevenly levelled competitions, frequent fluctuations in the currency, and high-level of corruption. The stability of the host country has always been of concern to businesses that operate internationally.

Obviously, the evaluation of a country's investment risks has an effect on the flow of FDI into the country. Nigeria should, therefore, pay attention to country risks evaluation because the lack of foreign capital inflow slows down the country's ability to pursue economic growth as well as create higher standard of living for its citizens.

Cost of production Inputs

The cost of production inputs is important because all organizations strive to have competitive advantages for themselves by reducing the cost of doing business. Countries that have low costs in labor and materials return higher margins of profits to investors. The goal of sourcing from low cost countries is, therefore, to bestow competitive advantages on the concerned organizations. Organizations and investors would, hence, go to any length to avail themselves of the opportunities offered by low cost countries.

The labor-oriented low cost factors include; the availability of the required skills, the cost of labor, and the labor reserve. The availability of the required skill and the cost of labor are very much essential to the location of an industry, and are thus, important considerations in siting an industry. For instance, before now, Mexico was the attraction for the United States companies by virtue of its cheaper labor and proximity to the American market. These organizations set up factories or went into partnership with companies from Mexico to avail themselves of the advantages of the cheap labor costs in the country. However, as soon as cost of production became cheaper in China, these companies left Mexico and moved in droves to China. For that reason, between 2002 and 2004, Mexico lost an estimated 400,000 jobs to China[10]. That China had low material costs was probably why between the years 2001 and 2002, China and its territories became the largest destination for inward FDI, attracting over $666 billion dollars[11]. FDI are, therefore, most likely to go to countries that give higher returns on investment.

The legal framework

The consideration for the legal framework includes the analysis of judicial independence; impartial courts; protection of intellectual property; lack of political interferences, and the integrity of the legal system. Generally the court systems in Nigeria are not very independent and lack impartiality. The previous military coups and the lack of protection of intellectual property tend to reduce the integrity of the legal systems.

Nigeria does not have legislation that offers adequate protection for property and contractual rights, and law enforcement is also often poor; the judicial processes are often slow and usually subjected to political interferences[12]. To stimulate FDI, Nigeria would need to improve its legal system;

as well as reduce bureaucratic bottlenecks, and improve its infrastructure. The weaknesses of the judiciary in Nigeria have continued to undermine the rule of law and would probably remain a concern and deterrent to would-be foreign investors.

Intellectual property protection

Modern day businesses are essentially driven by knowledge, information, and technology. Hence, the extent to which intellectual property is protected in a country is pertinent. Most intellectual property protection laws seek compliance with the Trade-Related Aspects of Intellectual Property (TRIPS) agreement of the Uruguay round of General Agreement on Trades and Tariffs (GATT).

An efficient judiciary system would enhance property rights by enforcing such rights[13]. For instance, the United States-based investors are not likely to invest in countries that fail to meet the threshold of effective governance in regulatory and legal systems that guarantee freedom of transactions, property rights, and   transparency of government processes [14].

Infrastructural and Geographical factors

The other inducements to attract FDI include quality of infrastructure, size and growth of domestic market, quality of labor force and the accessibility of the location[15]. The World Economic Forum had, however, reported that the reductions in costs of transportation and communications have reduced the importance of location; thereby, encouraging companies to embrace lower costs, political stability, and skilled labor as the drivers of competitiveness[16].

Chapter 17

The Trend of Foreign Direct Investment Inflow to Nigeria

Generally, natural resources, large markets good infrastructures, an educated population, openness to FDI, less corruption, political stability, and reliable legal systems will have positive impacts on FDI into such Sub-Saharan African (SSA) countries as Nigeria[1]. The assumption, however, has always been that countries with poor natural resources or small populations would not attract FDI irrespective of the policies such countries adopt[2]. As economic clusters influence the FDI inflows in such transitional economies as Nigeria, so also do market size, low cost of labour, and natural resources[3]. The total package of FDI, namely; technology, capital, management skills, and market linkages have, however, always lacked in Nigeria as in most developing countries[4].

For Nigeria, the common perception is that the FDI into country has been mineral-based; largely influenced by the availability of natural resources and large market size[5]. Nigeria could attract non-oil-based FDI by improving its policy and institutional environments. For instance, creating regional bloc would expand the market size; hence creating more attraction for FDI.

The trends of FDI flow in Nigeria have been on investments linked to natural resources, and domestic market sizes. Most of the FDI to Nigeria are natural resource-based; with the oil and the other natural resource been the main factor in the attraction of FDI into the country[6]. This is because the return on investment is highest in the petroleum sector[7].

Similarly, those Sub-Saharan African countries that have attracted the most FDI are those that have such large tangible assets as natural resources and large domestic markets[8]. For instance, three-quarters of the investment in natural resources of the SSA are held by companies in France, Japan, United Kingdom and the United States; mostly in the oil exporting countries of Nigeria and Angola[9]. About 60% of the FDI in Sub-Saharan Africa is allocated to oil and natural resources[10].

Notwithstanding significant risks, such countries as Angola, Botswana, Namibia and Nigeria have received substantial FDI targeted at oil and mineral sectors[11]. This is because the extractive industries involved are in remote areas, making the general lack of infrastructures in these countries unimportant[12]. Hence, despite its lack of infrastructure and other adverse factors Nigeria still receives a substantial amount of FDI, but only in the mineral extractive industries[13].

The other potential attracting factor of FDI into Nigeria is the availability of large domestic market. The size of the domestic market is not solely on population; but rather, requires the power to purchase, which is reflected by the country's income per capita. For instance, with a population of about 50million (against Nigeria's 150 million), South Africa has a domestic market three times greater than that of Nigeria, and thus attracts much more non-natural resource-based FDI[14].

Other potential trends of FDI inflows into Nigeria include investments linked to such incentives as export processing zones. The export-related industries, aided by the creation of export processing zones have attracted a measure of FDI in such countries as Mauritius[15]. Other countries as Mozambique and Uganda have also experienced notable successes in attracting FDI mainly because of policy reforms[16].

Chapter 18

Constraints to Foreign Direct Investment into Nigeria

Although, Foreign Direct Investment (FDI) gives more resources, facilitates technology and managerial transfers to host nations, the main constraints to FDI into Nigeria are the deficiency of infrastructure, weak public institutions, and lack of skilled labor[1]. The probability that foreign investors would get the required level of returns on their investment is also paramount[2]. More so, the availability of physical and human infrastructure, and the level of income per capital are reflective of the levels of economic development[3]. Higher levels of these factors are likely to be more attractive to investors; but unfortunately, Nigeria has long experienced the lower levels of these factors. The lack of the skill and technological capacity to absorb large FDI inflows are also constraints to investing in Nigeria[4].

In Nigeria, the constraint to FDI would include: political instability; weak infrastructure; the lack of the conducive legal and regulatory environments; concerns for public safety and rule of law; bureaucratic bottlenecks; high prevalence of corruption; constant policy reversal and uncertainty; lack of technological orientation, and low human capital. Generally, the removals of the impediments to private business activities are key drivers of FDI.

Lack of Conducive legal and regulatory Environment

The legal system of a country affects the conduct of business within the country. A business that desires to enter a country needs to know if the country's host government will be able to protect foreign businesses with an adequate legal system and not subject the legal environment of business to the whims and caprices of political leaders[5]. The legal issues here will include the protection or not of intellectual property rights.

Generally, the risks involved in investing in another country are thoroughly assessed. This is especially so when the economic and legal systems are entirely different from the home country. Such supportive institutional environments as effective legal systems, effective bureaucratic systems and financial systems are important for investment locations[6].

Weak infrastructures

A well-developed system of infrastructure is essential in attracting foreign capital and triggering economic growth. Well-developed infrastructures reduce transaction costs, and improve market access in the manufacturing and service sectors[7]. The productivities of investments are likely increased by good infrastructures; which thereby, stimulate the flow of FDI[8]. Whereas the determinants for investment in service sector are influenced by the availability of human capital, investment in manufacturing are influenced by good infrastructures[9].

Except for South Africa and Mauritius, most countries in Sub-Saharan Africa lack the basic infrastructures required to attract FDI. For that, in the Sub-Saharan Africa, South African is the highest beneficiary of FDI. Ninety percent of the investment into South Africa in the last decade came from the United Kingdom, Australia and the United States with the major investors as Mercedes-Benz and BMW of Germany[10]. One major reason for this is that South Africa has the best-developed infrastructure in Africa. The transportation infrastructure for mainstream business is well-developed; sizeable and efficient ports, excellent road network, and good air links; particularly to Europe and the United States[11]. Although good infrastructure is not very necessary for the extractive industries that constitute its main FDI, Nigeria needs to improve its infrastructure to attract the non-natural resource based investments[12].

Political Instability

The stability of the host country is usually an issue of good concern to any business that operates internationally. Political stability has, therefore, remained the most important determinant of the FDI into Africa[13]. Political risks are the possibility that political decisions, events or conditions in country would affect business environment in such a manner that investors would lose money or have lower than expected profit margins[14]. Except in cases of high endowment in natural resources and large domestic markets, countries that benefit from FDI are considerably politically stable. Such countries would usually have political stability; with a low risk of internal armed conflict.

Nigeria has a perception for political and economic instability, social strife, and weak governance[15]. Unfortunately, investors have become increasingly sensitive to economic and political instabilities; preferring to invest in countries with environments that are conducive to foreign investments[16].

Political stability is likely to be the greatest concern when considering the viability of any project in Nigeria. When opportunities are determined to be high and the risk factors low, the investment is likely to be acceptable. Hence, considering that countries compete for foreign investments, an investor is likely to prefer a country with less political instability and market uncertainty.

Concerns for Public Safety

There can probably be little or no economic growth or development without the basic security[17]. The function of the state with respect to internal security is not only to enhance security by lowering crime rates, but also enable citizens to resolve their differences without resorting to arms or physical coercion. The delivery of public and political goods becomes more feasible only when reasonable provisions for public safety and security have been made and obtained. Obviously, there are high concerns for public security and safety in Nigeria.

Bureaucratic bottlenecks

The bureaucratic consideration for a country includes existence of price controls issues, administrative obstacles for new business, time spent with government bureaucracy, ease of starting anew business and the enforceability of contracts. Obviously, bottlenecks exist in enforcing contracts, starting a new business or exiting a business in Nigeria. In Nigeria, excessive bureaucratic delays and such similar situations present some impediments to the smooth execution of economic projects. For instance, in the United States, it takes about one hour to register a business in a county, and about 20 minutes to completely process a business incorporation (online); takes one day in New Zealand; about three days in Singapore and Hong Kong, six days in South Korea, Denmark, Mauritius, and Malaysia; 12 days in United Kingdom; 14 days in Ghana; 19 days in South Africa; but 28 days in Nigeria[18].

High prevalence of Corruption

The analysis of the extent of corruption in Nigeria would involve the regulatory quality, the rule of law, and the control of corruption. The lacks of the political will to control corruption and the non-enforcement of regulations have remained the major bottlenecks to curbing corruption in Nigeria. Foreign firms operating in Nigeria indicate that bribery is a component of business and that bureaucratic corruption is an operational administrative order[19]. The high incidence of corruption creates inefficiency and makes the operating environment difficult for business.

Lack of Technological orientation

A pertinent consideration in investing in Nigeria could include the absence of the required technology orientation, the required technology infrastructure, and technological readiness;

as well as the absence of related and complimentary industries. This low technological capacity and orientation have had adverse effects on the efforts made toward the development of Nigeria. The technological deficiencies also prevent Nigeria from deriving the full benefits of FDI. The absence of human capital development negatively affects the diffusion of the benefits of FDI into the country. To increase the volume of FDI inflows, therefore, the Nigeria would need to improve its technological human capital capabilities as the country lacks the skill and technological capacity to absorb large FDI inflows[20].

Constant Policy Reversal and Uncertainty

Policy uncertainty has a negative impact on private investment because most of the costs are sunk and therefore irreversible[21]. Hence higher returns may not be high enough to compensate for loss that could arise from policy reversal. The uncertainty of government policies is therefore a contributory factor to the adverse risk assessment of the Nigerian investment environment.

Low human capital

The availability of human capital also has effects on the attractiveness of a country to Foreign Direct Investment. In order to increase the volume of FDI inflows, a country would need to improve their human capital capabilities[22]. Unfortunately, the presence of cheap and abundant labor in some countries like Nigeria seems to preclude the need for improved productivity[23].

Essentially, the availability of physical, infrastructure, human capital, and high income per capital are reflective of the levels of economic development[24]. To increase the volume of non-oil-based FDI inflows, Nigeria should follow the example of India by improving the human capital capabilities in the country, through education.

Chapter 19

Corruption: The Elephant in the Room

United Nations Development Program (UNDP) defines corruption as the abuse of power for private benefit through bribery, extortion, influence peddling, nepotism, fraud, or embezzlement[1]. Transparency International, the world-acclaimed organization on levels of corruption within nations, describes corruption as the 'abuse of entrusted power for private gain[2]. Corruption is more prevalent and acutely felt in such less developed countries as Nigeria where political institutions are weak and more vulnerable; and official procedures and safeguards less robust and less transparent.

The general effect is that a major portion of the scarce public fund and resources is diverted into private pockets, thereby exacerbating the poverty among the people. The much-needed public funds for these socioeconomic infrastructures are constantly and systematically siphoned and hidden in local and foreign bank accounts[3]. By syphoning the scarce resources that could be used to improve infrastructure, bolster the education systems, and strengthen public health, corruption stifles development[4].

Corruption in Nigeria is essentially a conspiracy of the elites. Rather than invest the mineral resource revenues into infrastructure and education, Nigerian leaders, often in collusion with exploration companies, siphon proceeds from the country's resources into their own pockets. Nigerian elites are not outraged or embarrassed by the level of corruption in the country. Rather, they bide their time, position themselves, and wait for own opportunities for corrupt enrichment.

A major constraint to the development of Nigeria is, therefore, the prevalence of political and bureaucratic corruption. Corruption in Nigeria is endemic, and the country has been consistently indexed by Transparency International as one of the most corrupt countries in the World. Corruption is highly detrimental to Nigeria as it leads to misallocation of resources, disrupts economic development and distorts public policies. The political and bureaucratic elites embezzle from national treasury for personal use, thereby undermining the accumulation of financial capital resources needed for economic development. The corruption is, therefore, not only detrimental to the society; but to business as well[5].

Similarly, the World Bank identifies corruption as the greatest obstacle to development because it distorts the rule of law and weakens the foundations of public institutions[6]. The International Monetary Fund (IMF) has also determined that countries with high corruption levels have less of their GPD going into investment[7]. This is because, corruption slows down economic development, stifles productive investment, escalates the cost of business, as well as the cost of public projects; and all these vices are capable of repressing national development. The problem of corruption in Nigeria extends through all layers of bureaucracy, including customs, police and the security and defence organs of the government[8]. Although, a weak rule of law reigns within the country, the lack of the political will to control corruption and the non-enforcement of regulations remain major problems.

Corruption does not only undermine investment and economic growth, it also aggravates poverty as even the poor have to bribe to obtain basic services in Nigeria. The corruption-prone and compromised public institutions share a large portion of the blame for the disappointing economic performances and poor developmental strategies that have continued to bestride the country.

The business elites also collude with the bureaucratic and political elites to embezzle from the national treasury, thereby, undermining the accumulation of financial resources needed for the development of welfare-enhancing projects. This corruption has adverse effects on national development as it stalls economic activities and development; and deters productive investment as resources are likely to flow out to other countries in which the investment climates are more favorable. Obviously, such vices slow down the process of national development.

Essentially, a state in which corruption is prevalent would suffer in relations to modernization because the personalized distributions of state resources to cronies are leveraged over the welfare-enhancing public goods and services. Generally, any country that is characterized by widespread personalization of power and massive corruption is not likely to experience sustainable development[9].

The major impediments to curbing corruption in Nigeria include the low risk of detection and punishment; the absence of a unified national value-system, and the lack of political will to curb corruption. By virtue of the differentials in culture and religion; and hence the absence of unified national value, different segments of the population perceive corruption differently. Usually, therefore, the meaningful fights against corruption have always assumed ethnic biases. The lack of the commitment of political leaders to its eradication is another impediment to the fight against corruption. Although, the concept of rule of law exists in the country, this lack of the political will to curb corruption, as well as the non-enforcement of existing regulations remain major problems.

Corruption in Nigeria can be curbed if political leaders are willing to impartially embark on such anti-corruption strategies as reducing and streamlining regulations to reduce opportunities for corruption, increasing bureaucratic checks and balances, and increasing the potentials for detecting and punishing corrupt officials. A number of countries that had similar high prevalence of corruption as Nigeria were able to curb corruption by adopting policies that reduced bureaucracy and reinforced the detection and sanctioning capacities against corruption.

PART VI

Policy Reforms for Development

Chapter 20

Creating the Environment for Foreign Direct Investment

Like every other, the governments of Nigeria should always be mindful of the need to attract foreign investment into the country. To attract more diversified Foreign Direct Foreign (FDI), the governments in Nigeria must, through public policies, make new and sustainable efforts to improve the investment climates. Obviously, both policy and institutional factors are determinants of FDI flows to a country[1]. From the institutional perspective, such positive outcomes of genuine political systems as reducing social and ethnic tensions by respecting the sovereignty, and electoral desires of the people have positive effects of the flow of FDI. For instance, part of the gains in the economic development of Mauritius was attributed to the political system that has established the basic institutional framework for organizing politics and governance to enhance inter-group relations and benefits[2]. This efficient and functioning political institutions that create good governance that contribute to transparency and accountability in government operations also create positive images to foreign investors[3]. Such countries as Mauritius, which have created opportunities for high levels of investment in freedom, property rights, business freedom, trade freedom, labor freedom, fiscal freedom, and freedom from government interference, have therefore, attracted a good measure of FDI[4]. As institutional factors are determinants of FDI flows, Nigeria would need to make the institutional changes that are required to create the right political environment.

The creation of a positive relationship between FDI and growth is, however, dependent on the foreign investment policies adopted by the host country. By focusing on correcting such issues as infrastructure deficiencies, regulatory and legal impediments, corruption, and other barriers that impede economic growth and market size, Nigeria would be able to attract more FDI. Even countries that are not endowed with natural resources have attracted FDI by improving their policy and institutional environments[5]. For Instance, despite smaller domestic markets and less abundance of natural resources, such countries as Mali and Mozambique have been successful in attracting FDI[6]. These countries achieved this success through policy reforms and high reputation for lower corruption levels and higher level of transparency in the conduct of public affairs; as well as making good efforts to create conducive investments and operational environment[7]. To stimulate FDI therefore, Nigeria would need to improve its legal system, reduce bureaucratic bottlenecks, and improve its infrastructure[8].

Obviously, modern strategic planning for global logistic networking is tied to the labor and transportation costs; infrastructure; business environment; nearness to market and suppliers; taxes and duties; and joint ventures. Nigeria could, therefore, attract more non-oil based FDI by improving the policy and institutional environments in the country. This is because; there is a relationship between a nation's policy and investment climate; and the level of its engagement into the global supply chain as determined by the amount of non-natural resource foreign investments. For instance, United States-based investors are not likely to invest in countries that fail to meet the threshold of effective governance in regulatory and legal systems that guarantee freedom of transactions, property rights, and transparency of government processes[9]. Other inducements to attract the American investors include quality of infrastructure, size and growth of domestic market, quality of labor force, and the accessibility of the location. The reductions in costs of transportation and communications have reduced the importance of location; thereby encouraging companies to embrace lower costs, political stability, and skilled labor as the drivers of competitiveness[10].

Some primary pathways to creating the climates for attracting FDI into Nigeria would include the formulation of state policies that are aimed at the diffusing the technologies and knowledge associated with the FDI. Another pathway would be the creation of the enabling environment for the diversification of FDI inflow to non-natural resource-based areas.

In considering such capital concerns as non-accessibility to the international capital market, and low saving rates; a viable route to poverty alleviation and development in Nigeria could, therefore be through FDI. This could be done if public policies are focused toward creating the platforms for the diversification of FDI to multiple sectors, the diffusion of the knowledge and technology from FDI, and the expansion of trading blocs. Nigeria can attract FDI through these policy measures; but to derive sustainable benefits from the inflow of FDI, the most important challenge is how to diffuse the technology and expertise into the society.

Diffusion of Technology and Knowledge

The trend of FDI into Nigeria concentrates on natural and mineral resource extractive industries that do not tend to generate such positive spillovers as technological transfers[11]. Public policies, designed primarily to ensure the diffusion of knowledge and technology should be formulated. Such policies would include identifying and supporting the developments of some priority projects that are capable of creating multiplier effects from the foreign investment projects; thereby helping to diffuse the initial technologies.

Another is, ensuring through policy instruments, that investing corporations have as close a technology-sharing affiliation as possible with their local suppliers. This would be necessary because, a channel for technological transfer is through close affiliation between the investing organizations and its local suppliers[12]. The magnitude of technological transfers would, however, be dependent on the technology gap between the foreign company and host country. The closer the development gap, the more the magnitude of technological likely to be transferred. The policy implication of this assertion is that Nigeria would be better served with FDI inflows from such more advanced developing countries such as Brazil, India, South Korea, Taiwan, and Mexico, than the developed countries: United States, Canada, Britain, France, or Germany.

Diversification of FDI into multiple sectors

The diversification of FDI into Nigeria would involve creating the enabling environment for the attraction of foreign investment into the non- natural resource sectors of the economy. Such countries as Tanzania, rich in mineral reserves with gold and diamonds have diversified into such areas as tourism; and by creating wildlife parks in 17 districts; Tanzania attracted more than 700,000 tourists in 2006 and a target of one million in 2010[13].

Expansion of Trading Blocs

Enlarging domestic markets by integrating national markets into larger trading areas has become a strategic option for nation-states. The necessities for regional economic integration are driven by such factors as the need for reduction in trade barriers, the attraction of FDI, economic competitiveness, and the need to forge new political geographies. The interconnected systems of today create high levels of transnational activity, both at regional and global levels[14]. The formation of trade blocs and the complete liberalization of trades and custom unification within and between the Sub-Saharan African trade blocs are imperative. The liberalization of tariff barriers among integrating economies should be a prominent feature of this regional system.

The formation of trade blocs in Sub-Saharan Africa would

reflect an emphasis on trade liberalization-the main economic aspect of globalization-but only at the regional level[15]. Trades and economic relationship are more mutually beneficial when done between countries with similar development problems and history. The need exists for the creation of such larger and functional regional markets as the South Africa Development Community (SADC). Creating regional bloc would expand the market size; and hence create more attraction for FDI[16]. Functional regional markets for the West African countries will open up a market with 300 million populations. Regional blocs could promote political stability (and curb coup d' tat) by restricting membership to only democratically elected government. Such blocs could also impose such conditions as curbing corruption, curbing crimes, and creating bureaucratic efficiencies. The creation of functional regional blocks would be very beneficial to the development of the Nigeria.

Chapter 21

The Use and Benefits of Export Processing Zones

A factor that could enhance the economic growth of a country is increasing the export potentialities of the country. To create the export potentialities, a country's export product would need to be competitive in foreign markets; both in terms of quality and price. With stable economic and liberal trade environments, Export Processing Zones (EPZs) have been successful in attracting FDI and expanding the export potentialities of a country.

Obviously, countries that actively promote foreign investment through EPZs or through internal regulations that make it easy for international businesses to operate will likely attract FDI. The attraction of FDI into the export processing zones of a country will usually contribute to economic development. The expected spillovers from the FDI would include the creation of employment and technological development of local industries.

An EPZ should enjoy the benefits of the good road

networks, an adjoining deep-water seaport, and an international airport; with the possibilities of linkages to other adjoining economic clusters. The EPZ should also, offer such incentives as complete tax holidays; and one-stop facilities for approval for permits, licenses and incorporation. Other incentives should include free duty on importation of goods, machinery and equipment. The laws setting up the EPZ could also grant 100% foreign ownership and 100% repatriation of earnings. Having already-built factory spaces that come with free rents for the first year reduces the financial requirement for the start-up capital. The EPZ should be available to both foreigners and citizens who are interested in investing and producing goods for the export market.

The possibility of restructuring the global production system; enhanced by the dispersal of manufacturing capacity to the developing countries would enable more countries industrialize. For instance, despite the smallness of market sizes and the lack of natural resources such countries as Mauritius and Seychelles have benefited from inflows of FDI by creating export platforms in the forms of EPZs.

The potentials and benefits of establishing multiple EPZs in Nigeria include: faster time to the consumer market, low cost of Production, and friendly investment climates for information technology.

The Time to market Advantages

With the EPZs located on the coastal cities of Nigeria, the obvious time-to market advantages exist over such low cost countries as China in relation to the American and European markets. For instance, the estimated cost of transporting a cell phone from Nigeria to the United States is about 10 cents if air freighted and 5 cents if shipped by sea; whereas the cost of transportation from China to the United States, if shipped by sea, is 14 cents and if by air is 71 cents[1].

In addition, the shipping time from China to the United States is between 21 to 23 days[2] as opposed to about 14 days from Nigeria. The proximity to the markets means less delivery times in which orders could be filled more quickly than the more distant suppliers.

Low cost of Production

One of the main reasons of the attraction of FDI to China is the low cost of production, especially in labor; making China one of the fastest growing markets in the world. China, therefore, returns a higher margin of profits to investors. Apparently, this is why between the years, 2001 and 2002, China and its territories became the largest destination for inward FDI, attracting over $666 billion dollars[3]. The abundance of cheap labour in the immediate environments of the EPZs would bear potentials for low cost advantages in Nigeria.

Good Climate for Investing In Information Technology

The creation and communication of knowledge have become the new tools for wealth and job creation[4]. The Information Technology (IT) industry has become the key ingredient for the development of a knowledge-based economy[5]. India and Taiwan have proven that a developing country can successfully industrialize through the high-tech sector.

The government of Mauritius government has also created an IT free-trade zone on the island; and it is expected that the IT zone will create thousands of jobs on the island. The government hopes to emulate the success of its Export Processing Zone (EPZ). In Nigeria, for instance, the city of Calabar, with its low crime level, geographical location as a sea port, the closeness to technical institutions, and the availability of export facilities makes it a good site for investments in information technology (IT).

Chapter 22

Policies for Foreign Direct Investments into Export Processing Zones

Nigeria has not yet convinced the non-mineral resource foreign investors to engage in non-natural resource activities. Part of the problem stems from a long history of anti-foreign investor policies. Even the existing 25 Free Trade Zones (FTZs) in Nigeria have not attracted non-oil-based FDI because of lack of investor-friendly environments, which, permeates the entire country. The need, therefore, exists for the government to change this image through full implementations of investor-friendly policies, as well as aggressive public relations efforts. Such policies must not only be aimed at developing the local market but also at the regional and global markets.

With the appropriate policy reforms in Nigeria, the country would be able to attract non-natural resources-based FDI. This could be achieved by designing the policies that are most likely to link the trade zone to the global supply chain system. Successes from such policy reforms have been experienced in India, Ireland, Singapore, Mauritius, and Taiwan.

The locations that have the potentials for development as EPZs include Calabar, Eket, Opobo, Bonny, Brass, Akasa, Port Harcourt, Oguta, Warri, Lekki, and Lagos. The policies to attract foreign investors to the EPZs would include; emphasizing investor-friendly mode of entry, transparency in investment, establishing One-Stop processing centers abroad, investment in human capital development, and encouraging tourism.

Emphasizing Investor-friendly Mode of Entry

Easing the modes of entry for foreign investors is an important policy instrument for attracting FDI. Usually, the modes of entry for FDI range from franchising, contractual arrangements (like licensing), stock investments, joint ventures, or direct investment. The direct foreign investment could involve setting a local manufacturing facility or by acquiring an existing manufacturer. Setting up a local manufacturing facility has the advantage of creating new jobs locally; and creating better relationship with the host country's government, customers, and local suppliers. The governments must design policies that ease the entry of investors; such as the reduction or removal of bureaucratic delays and bottlenecks.

The advantages stable legal and bureaucratic systems will provide would include the sustainable and stable development strategies and actions that are likely to facilitate foreign investment and internal economic growth. In such success stories as Mauritius, the environment is business-friendly, and licensing procedures are simple.

Transparency in Investment

Transparency in investment refers to necessity for a complete disclosure of all aspects of an investment to intending investors. That much transparency does not exist in the business world of Nigeria is an impediment; especially in stock investment. To be successful, the policies and procedures governing the EPZs should be of higher levels of transparency than the current levels in Nigeria. Such countries as Botswana that has one of the lowest corruption index in Africa; and whose corruption index is comparable to the countries of the European Union and the United States[1]; has hence, been one of the most recipients of FDI in the Sub-Saharan Africa. In Mauritius, another country with success stories; commercial operations are efficient; the judiciary is transparent and independent of politics; relatively free of corruption and able to protect property rights[2].

Establishing One-Stop Processing Centers Abroad

The creation of one-stop information and processing center for immigration, custom clearances, expatriate quotas, business registration and the approval of licenses in selected cities abroad, and manned by Nigerians living abroad, would be a strategic imperative. Investors could, then, process most of the necessary documentations before traveling to Nigeria; thereby avoiding the usual bureaucratic delays and corruption. The embassies abroad cannot do this job effectively because, for all intents and purposes, they are extensions of Nigeria's ineffective and corrupt bureaucracies.

Investment in Human Capital Development

In the global economy of today, it critical to employ, train, develop and retain employees who not only have the technical expertise but do also possess global knowledge and experiences. The institutions around the EPZ should be encouraged to create training and skill development programs to enhance the labour pool of the EPZ.

Encouraging Tourism

The EPZs should have the potentials of creating the enabling environments for diversification into tourism and its complimentary hospitality and entertainment industry. According to the 2004 World Tourism Organization report, about 25% of the world tourists are attracted to wildlife, 10% to site seeing, 40% to beaches and water sports, 10% mountaineering, 10% to gaming at resorts, and 5% to other attractions[3].

The EPZs would need investments in some of such sectors as world-class hotels, resorts, water-sport facilities, cableways, gabling facilities, airlines and charters, and any other important facilities that are attractive to tourists: swimming facilities, tennis courts, golf courses, racing facilities for horses, and many others.

Chapter 23

Macro- and Micro-Reforms

Macroeconomic (macro) reforms, such as, Foreign Direct Investments (FDI) and Export Processing Zones (EPZ) are externally-oriented reforms that are designed to open up a country's economic system to outside nations. Macro-reforms have long been going on in Nigeria in forms of export-oriented and market-oreinted strategies that are based on the privatization of state companies; currency adjustments and deregulation of the financial markets; reduction or removal of subsidies; and the lowering of tariffs. These strategies are obviously desirable as they could be vehicles for economic development, as well forces for ushering in new ideas and technologies. These wholesale reforms, as they are sometimes called, however, do not in themselves, induce sustainable development.

To create and sustain the development of nations, these macroeconomic reforms must be followed by the micro-reforms. The difference between macro and micro reforms is the former is much more externally-oriented; whereas the latter is more internally-oriented. In addition, whereas macro-reforms can be done by a few people using administrative fiats, micro-reforms require a wider commitment of the public and the willingness of the legislative arm of government to overcome the vested and entrenched interest of the political and economic elites. The 2008 Nobel Prize winner in economics, Paul Krugman, urges for more institutional and macro-economic inputs, as well as reforms; arguing that the economic growth of the East Asian countries was as a result of the use of more inputs rather than use of innovations[1].

Tom Friedman in, *The World is Flat: A brief History of the Twenty-First Century*, indicates that micro-reforms involve infrastructure, regulatory institution, education, and the cultural orientation of the society[2]. The idea of these micro-reforms is to create the legal and institutional frameworks and environments that enable the greatest number of citizens to innovate, start companies, and become entrepreneurs, and collaborate with the outside world[3]. Countries can, therefore, manage large portions of their population out of poverty; not only by embarking on such macro-reforms as changes in fiscal and monetary policies, but also by creating such micro-reforms that enable the people to raise capitals and start businesses under competitive conditions[4].

According to the World Bank's International Finance Corporation (IFC), the core criteria for micro-reforms are: (i) the ease of starting a business in terms of rules, regulations, and fees; (ii) the ease of hiring and firing; (iii) the ease of enforcing contract; (iv) the ease of getting a credit; and (v) the ease of closing a business[5].

A comparison of the practices in Nigeria with some other

countries in relation to these core criteria will be helpful in understanding the need for these micro-reforms in Nigeria. For instance, as the IFC indicates, it takes six days to start a business in Mauritius, Denmark, and South Korea; but 28 days in Nigeria[6]. It takes no monetary cost to start a business in Denmark; 0.3% of the per capita income in New Zealand, United Kingdom, and South Africa; equal or less than 1.5% in United States, Norway, Botswana, Hong Kong, and Singapore; but 58.3% of per capita income in Nigeria[7]. A simple commercial contract takes 150 days to enforce in Singapore; 216 days in New Zealand; 270 days in the United States; 280 days in Norway; but 450 days in Nigeria[8]. Private credit agencies have the credit history of almost every adult in New Zealand, Norway, and the United states; 60.7% in Botswana; 55.6% in South Africa; but virtually none in Nigeria[9]. In the United States, Canada, Britain, New Zealand and such other countries, laws on bankruptcy and collateral give the creditors the required power to recover their money when a debtor defaults, a creditor in Nigeria does not have such a leverage[10].

Essentially, the IFC advises governments to deregulate and encourage competition; focus on enhancing property rights; expand the use of internet for regulation fulfillment, so as to make the process more open and transparent, and less susceptible to bribery; and reduce court involvement in business matters[11]. The other aspects of micro-reforms should include the expansion of educational opportunities as well the expansion of such logistic infrastructure as roads, sea ports, air ports, and telecommunications.

In addition, there is need to address those cultural orientations of the society which have become adversarial to development. As David Landes argues in, *The Wealth and Poverty of Nations*, although climates, natural resources, and geography all play crucial roles in the development of nations, the key factor is a country's cultural endowments and orientation[12]. The cultural endowment relates to the degree to which a country embraces the values of hard work, honesty, patience, tenacity, delayed gratification, openness to change and new technology. Nations develop when the citizens have a sense of national solidarity that focuses on development; when stranger-citizens can have the trust to collaborate together; and when the elites show concern for the poor masses, and are therefore ready to invest at home rather that invest abroad[13]. On individual levels, hard work, strong family bonds, and devotion to education can create boundless opportunities.

The cultural re-orientation that works to reduce the power distance in a society also contributes to enhance the prospects of national development. Power distance refers to the manner a societies addresses physical, material and intellectual inequalities within its structure and politic. Power distance reflects the level at which people are comfortable with inequalities in the wielding of power among institutions and people[14] . This dimension indicates how a society stratifies its individuals and groups with respect to power, authority, prestige, status, wealth and other material possessions[15].

Some cultural types allow inequalities to grow over time until there is great separation of power and wealth, whereas others attempt to minimize the inequalities by redistributing power and wealth[16]. The cultural types that allow inequalities to grow are termed high power distance, while those that minimize inequalities are termed low power distance[17]. In low power distance societies, individuals strive for power equalization and justice. The low power distance Anglo-American, Nordic, and Germanic cultures place more emphasis on competence than on seniority. These cultures minimize inequalities, favor less autocratic leaders, and favor less centralization of authority.

High power distance societies are usually status-conscious, respecting age and seniority, bestowing outward importance on protocol, formality, and hierarchy. Very high power distance societies as Nigeria accept and support large imbalances in power, status, and wealth; much respect is shown for those in authority; and titles, ranks, and status are revered. These cultures have greater acceptance for inequalities and authoritarian leadership. Governments must, therefore, make concise efforts to reduce the culture of accepting inequalities in the society by reducing the gaps in the privileges, positions, and wealth among the citizens.

Essentially, the prospects of national development for less developed countries rest on macro-reforms; followed by micro-reforms that encompass good governance, education, infrastructure, and ability to embrace technological changes. Obviously, a country's ability and willingness to sacrifice and work together for economic development; as well as the presence of national leadership with the required visions to use its power for development, rather than for personal enrichment; all create sustainable national development.

Chapter 24

Instituting a Well-defined Private Property System

A private property can be defined as "the legal right to exclude others from the resources that are originally possessed or acquired without force, theft, or fraud"[1]. In a democracy, the property system is the "system of law under which state recognizes and enforces the rights of the individual to acquire, possess, use, and transfer scarce resources"[2]. Under this system, the people themselves determine what is worthy of acquisition, and through the exchange of money or any other thing of value, acquire the resources they need. The role of the state becomes to legally recognize when any individual has exclusive property rights, and allow the individual use or enforce such rights through some administrative systems or the court system.

Private properties would among others, include such things as land, houses, automobiles, corporate shares and stocks, market stalls, and even one's labour. These rights and ownership can be recognized by the issuance of titles of ownership of the resource as in automobiles; or by the issuance of deeds of ownership as in lands. Although, the state may have the power of eminent domain over private property, that power should only be exercised after the payment of a fair and just compensation. Eminent domain refers to the power of the government to force private property owners to exchange their resources, especially land, for money, for public uses[3]. Property rights and laws do not, however, function well when they are not adequately enforced by an honest police that is needed to deter the robbery, theft, or fraud; and impartial judges that are required to resolve the disputes that arise over ownership[4].

The protection of private property rights is of immense importance as the main basis for the economic development in the western world seems to be a well-developed property rights system; as economic specialization, which is the main ingredient of modernization, requires well-defined property rights[5]. The capitalist and free market systems are, therefore, essentially a legal property system.

As Hernando De Soto indicated in, *The mystery of capital: Why capitalism triumphs in the West and fails everywhere else*, the characteristics that the third world countries have in common is a very underdeveloped property rights system and the lack of the legal apparatus for protecting and enforcing property rights[6]. The cause of underdevelopment in most third world countries is, therefore, essentially a legal system that does not allow the majority to accumulate capital, to organize value, or even to transfer it[7]. In most third world and old communist countries, there seems to be a sort of legal apartheid that blocks the majority from wealth creation by not developing the legal property system that provides the framework for majority of the entrepreneurs[8]. It is noteworthy that under this De Soto's initiative, the government of Peru issued over 1.2 million property titles to urban squatters.

Private property is, therefore, central to building the environment that is conducive for business, as well as being central to the development of national and individual wealth. Taking an automobile for instance; an owner, can generate personal wealth by; driving to work or carrying out commercial activities; sell the car; rent the car to a taxi company; or use the car to secure a loan. An owner who uses his or her car to secure a loan generates wealth in two-fold; by investing the borrowed money and by still using the car to carry out wealth-generating activities. These are the cogent reasons why nations that desire to have sustainable development must have efficient and secured private property title system. This wealth must, however, be more easily transferable and made to have a fiduciary value by representing it on a paper called an "automobile title", which excludes others from interfering with these uses.

The benefits of a private property system include: (i) the promotion of incentives, (ii) the generation of prosperity, and (iii) the divisibility of prosperity.

(a)The promotion of incentives to produce

Private property motivates the efforts to produce more by allowing the individuals keep and benefit from what they produce. The individual produces more than he/she personally needs, and exchanges it through money for the other things of value owned by others; thereby creating more wealth, and distributing the wealth too.

(b)The generation of prosperity

By creating the enabling environment for capital formation, private property generates prosperity. With a legally recognized property such as a home, an individual can borrow money from a financial institution. While still living in the homestead, the individual uses the borrowed money to generate more wealth; thereby increasing his/her prosperity.

A lender is, however, only willing to extend such loans other certain conditions which are primarily that; (i) the borrower's property is physically identifiable and recognized by the state; (ii) the state recognizes the individuals claim to the ownership of the property; and (iii) the states permits the lenders to enforce the lending agreement through a legal system that includes the ability to sell the borrowers property if the borrower fails to repay the loan[9]. These conditions can only be created and protected by state, under a well-defined private property system.

(c) Encourages the divisibility of prosperity

By permitting properties to be broken down into parts, the private property system encourages the divisibility of prosperity. Under the private property system, an owner of a piece of land can sell a part of it on credit (and hold a mortgage to ensure payments); lease part of it to rent-paying tenants; incorporate part of it and sell shares to investors; or secure loan against part of it to invest in a business[10]. Each of these transactions creates divisibility of the prosperity accruable from the single piece of land. Each transaction is, however, only made possible where the property law enables private properties to be so subdivided as the owners deems and derives most advantages[11].

Essentially, the goal of a society is to produce more of what its people want or need, both at the individual and national level. The excess production is exchanged (sold) to other nations in form of exports; thereby creating wealth of both the state and the individuals. To achieve this, certain goals are necessary, the paramount being the existence of a well-defined private property system, as well as the equal application of the rule of law to all citizens.

Nigeria does not have strong and enforceable laws and regulations that offer adequate protection for property and contractual rights; and law enforcement is also often poor. These weaknesses in the judicial system in Nigeria have, therefore, continued to undermine the enforcement of property rights, and, therefore remain sources of concern, sometimes constituting blocks to would-be foreign investments.

Chapter 25

Technological Reforms for Take-off

Walt Whitman Rostow in the book, *The stages of Economic Growth,* indicated that a modern society develops along a trajectory that starts with a traditional society, preparing the pre-conditions of take-off, take-off stage, drive to maturity stage, and the age of high mass-consumption[1]. Rostow used this trajectory to identify the economic dimensions of all societies. A traditional society is that whose structure is developed within limited production functions in which there exists a ceiling on the level of attainable output per head[2]. Although, a very high percentage of Nigerians still live in traditional settings, Nigeria does seem to be at the second stage of development in which the pre-conditions for take-off are been developed.

As Walt Rostow postulates, in preparing for the take-off from traditional societies to modern societies, the fruits of modern science must be exploited to fend off the diminishing returns of human labour and embrace the technology and science of mass production in agriculture and industry[3]. This stage would involve enterprising in the private and public sectors, setting up financial institutions for mobilizing and investing capital; investment in transportation, communications, and the raw material or services that other nations may have an economic interest[4]. The indigenously created or adapted manufacturing processes appear, and the scope of internal and external commerce widens[5]. In this stage, new techniques spread in agriculture and industry. Agriculture is commercialized, bringing in the new changes in productivity that is an essential condition for successful take-off[6]. To create these pre-conditions for the take-off stage requires much input of technological prowess.

There are, however, three different kinds of ways a society can acquire the required technology to launch the take-off, namely; through patenting, transferring, or copying of technology. There are, therefore, three kinds of acquirable technologies: (i) patent technology, (ii) transfer of technology, and (iii) copy technology. Patent technologies are those inventions and innovation, which a society, through its resourcefulness and innovativeness develops for itself. Transfer of technology is the discredited concept that western companies espouse as they invest in some third world countries. Evidence has, however, shown that no technologies are transferred to the host nations. The fact remains that these technologies are the core competencies of these companies; and for reasons of continuous technological advantages, it does not serve the interests of these organizations to compromise their core competencies by 'transferring' them to companies in these developing countries. Moreover, arguments have been made that transfer of technology, mostly through foreign direct investments, is only effective when the necessary absorptive capacities have been developed; which is not the case in most of the developing countries.

The most reasonable technological perspective for Nigeria would be the copy technology, in which the governments invest in developing the human and material capital for the copying of existing technologies; only to the extent of avoiding copyright breaches. Most Asia countries have joined the league of developed nations by technologizing their societies and embarking on massive copy technology. To join the league of developing or developed nations, Nigeria must first create technology-friendly environments through investment in the practical application of technology; and then embarking on strategies for massive copy technology. India has no mineral resources, but has been able to anchor onto the global supply chain by educating a relatively large portion of its population in physical sciences, engineering, and medical sciences that enabled them copy existing technologies[7].

ENDNOTES

Chapter 1: Sovereignty of the People: The core of Democratic Governance
1. Rotberg, R. (2007). Governance and leadership in Africa, Broomal, PA: Mason Crest Publishers.
2. Ibid.
3. Ibid.
4. Ibid.
6. Foweraker, J. & Krznaric, R. (2001). How to construct a database of liberal democratic performance. Democratization, 8(3), 1-25.
7. LeVan, A. (2007). Dictators, democrats and development in Nigeria. A PhD Dissertation, University of California, San Diego. AAT 3283913.
8. Ibid.
9. Lake, D. & Baum, M. (2001).The Invisible hand of Democracy: Political control and the provision of Public Services. Comparative Political Studies, 34, 589-621.
10. Ibid.
11. Riker, W.H. (1993). Comments on Radcliff's "liberalism, populism and Collective Choice". Political Research Quarterly, Volume 46 (1). 143-149.
12. Asen, R. (2003). The Multiple Mr. Dewey: Multiple Publics and Permeable Borders in John Dewey's Theory of the Public Sphere. Argumentation and Advocacy, 39(3).
13. African Development Bank (2005). African Development Report, 2005.Oxford: Oxford University Press, p.197.
14. Diamond, L. (2008) The Spirit of Democracy: The struggle to build free Societies throughout the World. New York: Henry Holt.
15. United Nations (1966) International Covenant on Civil and Political Rights (ICCPR), United Nations General Assembly, New York.
16. Putnam, R. (2000). Bowling Alone: The Collapse and Revival of American Community. New York: Simon & Schuster.
17. Diamond, L. (2008) The Spirit of Democracy: The struggle to build free Societies throughout the World. New York: Henry Holt.
18. Cain, B.E. (1999). In Lipstz, K.L (2004). Campaigns and Competition: How to Enhance Voter Knowledge and Deliberation in Mass Democracy. Ph.D. Dissertation. University of California. Berkley, United States. AAT 3167206.
19. United Nations (1966) International Covenant on Civil and Political Rights, United Nations General Assembly, New York.
20. Lipset, S. M. (1963). Political Man: The social bases of politics. Garden City, NY: Double day & Company.
21. Tvinnereim, E. M. (2004). Democratic contestation, accountability and citizen satisfaction in German states. Paper presented at the annual Meeting of The Midwest Political Science Association, Palmar House Hilton, Chicago, Illinois.
22. LeVan, A. (2007). Dictators, democrats and development in Nigeria. A PhD

Dissertation, University of California, San Diego. AAT 3283913.

23. Tvinnereim, E. M. (2004). Democratic contestation, accountability and citizen satisfaction in German states. Paper presented at the annual Meeting of The Midwest Political Science Association, Palmar House Hilton, Chicago, Illinois.

24. Marshall, M.G & Cole, B.R. (2009). Global report 2009.Severn, MD: Center for systemic Peace.

25. Marshall, M.G & Cole, B.R. (2009). Global report 2009.Severn, MD: Center for systemic Peace.

26. Ibid.

27. Coa, F. (2009). Modernization theory and China's road to modernization. Chinese Studies in History, 43(1), p.8.

28. International IDEA (2008). Assessing the quality of democracy: An overview of the international IDEA framework. Stockholm: International IDEA.

Chapter 2: The Advantages of Democracy

1. Diamond, L. (2008) The Spirit of Democracy: The struggle to build free Societies throughout the World. New York: Henry Holt.

2. Gerring, J., Philip, B., Barndt, W. T. & Moreno, C. (2005). Democracy and economic growth: A historical perspective. World Politics, 57, 323-264.

3. Maynor, J. (2006). Modern republican democratic contestation: A model of deliberative democracy. In I. Honohan & J. Jennings, Republicanism in Theory and practice, 125-139. NY: Rout ledge.

4. Wright, J. (2008). Political competition and democratic stability in new democracies. B.J. Pol. S., 38, 221-245.

5. Diamond, L. (2008) The Spirit of Democracy: The struggle to build free Societies throughout the World. New York: Henry Holt.

6. Robert Dahl (2005). *Who Governs? Democracy and power in the American City.* New Haven, CT: Yale University Press

7. Ibid

8. Ibid

Chapter 3: Internal factors constraining democracy in Nigeria

1. Diamond, L. (2008) The Spirit of Democracy: The struggle to build free Societies throughout the World. New York: Henry Holt and Company, p.155.

2. Sandbrook, R. (1985). The Politics of Africa's Economic Stagnation. New York: Press Syndicate, Cambridge University Press.

3. Ibid

4. Ibid

5. Ekman, J. (2009). Political participation and regime stability: A framework for analyzing hybrid regimes. International Political Science Review. 30 (1), 7-31.

6. Levitsky, S. & Way, L.A. (2009). Competitive authoritarianism: The emergence and dynamics of hybrid regimes in the post-cold war era. New York, NY: Cambridge University Press.

7. Diamond, L. (2008) The Spirit of Democracy: The struggle to build free Societies throughout the World. New York: Henry Holt and Company, p.155.

8. Ibid, p.167).

9. Sandbrook, R. (1985). The Politics of Africa's Economic Stagnation. New York: Press

Syndicate, Cambridge University Press.

10. Rotberg, R. (2009). Governance and leadership in Africa: Measures, methods and results (Ibrahim index of African governance report). Journal of International Affairs, 62.

11. Okoye, I. (2007). Political godfatherism, electoral politics and governance in Nigeria. Paper presented at the 65th Annual Conference of MPSA held in Chicago, USA, April 12-15, 2007, p. 2.

12. Ikpe, U. B. (2009). The impact of manipulated re-elections on accountability and legitimacy of democratic regimes in Africa: Observations from Nigeria, Zambia and Kenya. African Journal of Political Science and International Relations, 3(7), pp. 300-310.

13. Ibid.

14. Ibid, p.301).

15. Ibid, p. 303).

16. Sandbrook, R. (1985). The Politics of Africa's Economic Stagnation. New York: Press Syndicate, Cambridge University Press.

Chapter 4: Analyzing the Modernization Model

1. Brinkman, R.L. (1995). Economic Growth versus Economic Development: Towards a Conceptual Clarification. Journal of Economic Issues, Volume 29(4), pp.1171-1188.

2. Wang, J. (2009). Some Reflections on Modernization Theory and Globalization Theory. Chinese Studies in History, Volume 43 (1), pp.72-98.

3. Cao, F. (2009). Modernization Theory and China's Road to Modernization. Chinese studies in History, Volume 43(1).

4. Yuan, P. (2009) Modernization Theory. Chinese studies in History, Volume 43(1), pp.37-45

5. Cao, F. (2009). Modernization Theory and China's Road to Modernization. Chinese studies in History, Volume 43(1).

6. Chen, E.K.Y. ((2005). Teaching and Learning Development Economics: Retrospect and Prospect. Journal of Economic Education, Volume 36(3).

7. Cao, F. (2009). Modernization Theory and China's Road to Modernization. Chinese studies in History, Volume 43(1).

8. Ibid.

9. Yuan, P. (2009) Modernization Theory. Chinese studies in History, Volume 43(1), pp.37-45

10. Hettne, B.(1983)The development of Development Theory. Acia Sociologica, 26(3/4), pp.247-266

11. Cao, F. (2009). Modernization Theory and China's Road to Modernization. Chinese studies in History, Volume 43(1).

12. Hosseini, H. (2003).Why Development is more complex Than Growth: clarifying some confusions. Review of social economy, LXI (1), pp. 93-110.

Chapter 5: Analyzing the Dependency Model

1. Heller, P. Rueschemeyer, D. & Snyder, R. (2009).Dependency and Development in a Globalized World: Looking Back and Forward. St Comp .Int. Dev. 44.pp.287-295.

2. Frank, A.G. (1975). On capitalist underdevelopment. London: Oxford University

Press.

3. Baran, P.A. (1957). The political economy of Growth. New York: Monthly Review.

4. Ibid

5. Rodney, W. (1982) How Europe Underdeveloped Africa. Washington, Dc: Howard University Press.

6. Ibid

7. Ibid.

8. Heller, P. Rueschemeyer, D. & Snyder, R (2009).Dependency and Development in a Globalized World: Looking Back and Forward. St Comp .Int. Dev. 44.pp.287-295.

9. Cardoso, F. & Faletto, E.(1979).Dependency and Development in Latin America. Berkeley: University of California Press.

10. Ibid

11. Ibid

12. Frank, A.G. (1975). On capitalist underdevelopment. London: Oxford University Press.

13. Cardoso, F. & Faletto, E. (1979).Dependency and Development in Latin America. Berkeley: University of California Press.

14. Shie, V.H. & Meer, C. D. (2010).The Rise of Knowledge in Dependency Theory: The Experience of India and Taiwan. Review of Radical Political Economics. 42(1), pp.81-99.

15. Wibbels, E. (2009). Cores, peripheries, and contemporary Political Economy. St Comp. Int. Dev. (2009). Volume 44.pp441-449.

16. Ibid.

17. Shie, V.H. & Meer, C. D. (2010).The Rise of Knowledge in Dependency Theory: The Experience of India and Taiwan. Review of Radical Political Economics. Vol. 42 (1), pp.81-99.

18. Ibid

19. Ibid.

20. Heller, P. Rueschemeyer, D. & Snyder, R. (2009).Dependency and Development in a Globalized World: Looking Back and Forward. St Comp .Int. Dev.44.pp.287-295.

21. Shie, V.H. & Meer, C. D. (2010).The Rise of Knowledge in Dependency Theory: The Experience of India and Taiwan. Review of Radical Political Economics. Vol. 42(1), pp.81-99.

22. Dos Santos, T. (1970). The structure of Dependence. American Economic Review. Volume 60(2), pp. 231-236.

23. Ibid.

24. Castells, M. & Laserna, R. (1994). The new dependency: Technological change and socioeconomic restructuring in Latin America. In comparative national development, ed. Kincaid, A.D. & Portes, A., pp.57-83.Chapel Hill: University of North Carolina Press.

25. Shie, V.H. & Meer, C. D. (2010).The Rise of Knowledge in Dependency Theory: The Experience of India and Taiwan. Review of Radical Political Economics. Vol. 42 (1), pp. 81-99.

CHAPTER 6: Lewis (Dual sector) model

1. Lewis, W.A. (1954). Economic Development with Unlimited Supplies of Labor.

Manchester School, 28(1), pp139-91. Reprinted in A. N. Agarvala and S.P. Singh (Eds), The Economics of Underdevelopment, Bombay: Oxford University Press.

2. Chen, E.K.Y. ((2005). Teaching and Learning Development Economics: Retrospect and Prospect. Journal of Economic Education, Volume 36(3).

3. Ibid.

4. Hettne, B. (1983). The development of Development Theory. Acia Sociologica, 26(3/4), pp. 247-266

5. Ibid

6. Lewis, W. A. (1996). Economic reform and political transition in Africa: The quest for a politics of development, World Politics, 49(1), pp. 92-129.

7. Ibid.

8. Chen, E.K.Y. ((2005). Teaching and Learning Development Economics: Retrospect and Prospect. Journal of Economic Education, Volume 36(3).

9. Ibid

10. Lewis, W.A. (1996). Economic reform and political transition in Africa: The quest for a politics of development, World Politics, 49(1), pp. 92-129.

11. Chen, E.K.Y. ((2005). Teaching and Learning Development Economics: Retrospect and Prospect. Journal of Economic Education, Volume 36(3).

12. Ranis, G. (2004). Arthur Lewis Contribution to Development Thinking and Policy. The Manchester School, Volume 72(6), pp.712-723.

13. Ibid.

14. Ibid.

15. Mosley, P. (2004) Institutions and Politics in a Lewis-Type Growth Model. The Manchester School. 72 (6).

16. Hettne, B. (1983) The development of Development Theory. Acia Sociologica, 26(3/4), pp.247-266

17. Mosley, P. (2004) Institutions and Politics in a Lewis-Type Growth Model. The Manchester School. 72 (6).

18. Ranis, G. (2004). Arthur Lewis Contribution to Development Thinking and Policy. The Manchester School, Volume 72(6), pp.712-723.

Chapter 7: Analyzing the other Development Models

1. Hettne, B. (1983). The development of Development Theory. *Acia Sociologica,* 26(3/4), pp. 247-266.

2. Yuan, P. (2009) Modernization Theory. Chinese studies in History, Volume, 43(1), pp.37-45.

3. Hettne, B. (1983). The development of Development Theory. *Acia Sociologica,* 26(3/4), pp. 247-266.

4. Ibid.

5. Rostow, W.W. (1960). The Stages of Economic Growth: A Non-Communist Manifesto. Cambridge, MA: The University Press.

6. Hettne, B. (1983). The development of Development Theory. *Acia Sociologica,* 26(3/4), pp. 247-266., p. 248.

7. Chen, E.K.Y. ((2005). Teaching and Learning Development Economics: Retrospect and Prospect. Journal of Economic Education, Volume 36(3).

8. Hettne, B. (1983). The development of Development Theory. *Acia Sociologica,*

26(3/4), pp. 247-266.

9. Hosseini, H. (2003).Why Development is more complex Than Growth: clarifying some confusions. Review of social economy, LXI (1), pp.93-110.

10. Barfield, T. (1997). The dictionary of anthropology. New York: Wiley-Blackwell.

11. Wallerstein, I (2004). A World-system perspective on the Social sciences. British Journal of Sociology, volume 61, pp. 167-177.

12. Ibid.

13 Hettne, B. (1983). The development of Development Theory. *Acia Sociologica, 26*(3/4), pp. 247-266

14. Heller, P. Rueschemeyer, D. & Snyder, R. (2009).Dependency and Development in a Globalized World: Looking Back and Forward. St Comp .Int. Dev. 44.pp.287-295.

15. Sherriff, P.E. (1983). State Theory, Social Science and Governmental Commissions. The American Behavioral Science, Volume 26(5)

16. Cardoso, F. & Faletto, E. (1979).Dependency and Development in Latin America. Berkeley: University of California Press.

17. Wallerstein, I (2004). A World-system perspective on the Social sciences. British Journal of Sociology, volume 61, pp.167-177.

18. Huang, X. (2005). The rise and fall of the East Asian growth system, 1951-2000. London: Routledge.

Chapter 8: The Conceptualizing Comparative Advantages

1. Pugel, T.A. (2004).International Economics.12Ed.New York: McGraw-Hill Companies.

2. Sutherland, P. (2007) Challenges to the Multilateral Trading System World *Economics.* Volume 8 (1). 1-14.

3. Nyahoho, E. (2010). Determinants of comparative in International trade of services: An Empirical Study of the Heckscher-Ohlin Approach. *Global Economy Journal,* Volume10 (1), article 3.

4. Ibid.

5. Krugman, P.R. & Obstfeld, M. (2006). *International Economics: Theory & Policy.*7th Ed. Boston: Darly Fox.

6. Ibid.

7. Olofin, S. (2002). Trade and Competitiveness of African Economies in the 21st Century. *Scottish Journal of Political Economy.*49 (5)

8. Fisch, G. & Speyer (1997). TRIPS as an adjustment Mechanism in North-South Trade. *Economics.*Vol. 55-56.

9. Chen, E.K.Y. ((2005). Teaching and Learning Development Economics: Retrospect and Prospect. Journal of Economic Education, Volume 36(3).

Chapter 9: The Conceptualizing Globalization

1. Wang, J. (2009). Some Reflections on Modernization Theory and Globalization Theory. Chinese Studies in History, Volume 43 (1), 72-98.

2. Ibid.

3. Ibid.

4. McAdams, T., Neslund, N., & Neslund, K. (2004). *Law, Business & Society.* New York: The McGraw-Hill Companies, p. 206

5. Gilpin, R. (1978). The Political Economy of International Relations. Princeton, New Jersey: Princeton University Press.P.389.In J. Mensah (2006). Cultural Dimensions of Globalization in Africa: A Dialectical Interpretation of Local and the Global. *Studies in Political Economy*, 77,57-83.

6. Kobrin, S. (1997). The Architecture of Globalization: State Sovereignty in a Networked Global Economy. In J. Mensah (2006). Cultural Dimensions of Globalization in Africa: A Dialectical Interpretation of Local and the Global. *Studies in Political Economy,* 77, 57-83.

7. Pugel, T.A. (2004).International Economics.12Ed.New York: McGraw-Hill Companies, p. 5.

8. Balls, D., McCulloch, W.H., Franz, P.L., Geringer, J.M., &Minor, M.S. (2005).International Business: *The Challenge of Global Competition*. New York: The McGraw-Hill Companies, p. 19.

9. Bhola H.S. (2003). Reclaiming Old Heritage for Proclaiming Future History: The Knowledge for Development Debate in African Context. In J. Mensah (2006). Cultural Dimensions of Globalization in Africa: A Dialectical Interpretation of Local and the Global. *Studies in Political Economy*, 77,

10. Balls, D., McCulloch, W.H., Franz, P.L., Geringer, J.M., &Minor, M.S. (2005).International Business: *The Challenge of Global Competition*. New York: The McGraw-Hill Companies.

11. Mensah, J. (2006). Cultural Dimensions of Globalization in Africa: A Dialectical Interpretation of Local and the Global. *Studies in Political Economy*, 77, p. 58.

12. Wibbels, E. (2009). Cores, peripheries, and contemporary Political Economy. *St Comp. Int. Dev.* (2009). Volume 44.pp. 441-449

13. Wang, J. (2009). Some Reflections on Modernization Theory and Globalization Theory. Chinese Studies in History, Vol. 43 (1), pp.72-98.

14. Ibid.

Chapter 10: Democracy and Development

1. Landman, T. (1999, p.607). Economic Development and Democracy: The view from Latin America, *Political Studies, XLVII.*

2. Feng, Y. & Zak, P.(1999).The determinants of Democratic Transitions, The Journal of Conflict Resolution, volume 43(2), p. 162.

3. Bratton, M. & Mattes, R. (2001).Africa's Surprising Universalism. Journal of Democracy, Volume 12(1), p. 117.

4. Przeworski, A, Alvarez, M. Cheibub, J, & Limongi, F. (2000). *Democracy and Development: Political Institutions and Material Well-being in the World, 1950-1990.*Cambridge, MA: Cambridge Press

5. Organski, A.F.K. (1973). The stages of political development. New York: Alfred A. Knopt.

6. Schraeder, P.J. (2004). *African politics and society: A mosaic in transformation.* New York: Thomson Belmont.

7.Feng,Y. & Zak, P.(1999).The determinants of Democratic Transitions, The Journal of Conflict Resolution, volume 43(2), p. 162.

8. Huntington, S.P. (1993). The Third Wave: Democratization in the Late 20th Century. Norman, OK: University of Oklahoma Press.

9. Landman, T. (1999). Economic Development and Democracy: The view from Latin America, *Political Studies, XLVII.*

10. Brown, D. (1999) Reading, Writing and Regime Type: Democracy's impact on Primary School Enrollment. Political Research Quarterly, Volume 52, pp. 681-707.

11. Boix, C. (2003). Democracy and Redistribution. Cambridge, MA; Cambridge University Press.

12. Schultz, P.T (1999).Health and Schooling Investment in Africa. Journal of Economic Perspectives, 13(3), pp.67-88.

13. Burkhart, R. & Lewis-Beck, M. (1994).Comparative Democracy: The Economic Development Thesis. The American Political Science Review, volume, 88(4), p. 907.

14. Kulger, J. & Feng. Y. (1999). Explaining and modeling Democratic Transitions. Journal of Conflict Resolution, Volume 43(2).

15. Lipset, S. M. (1959). Some Social requisites of democracy: Economic development and political Legitimacy. Bobbs-Merrill.

16. Ibid, p.71

17. Hedenius, A. (1992). Democracy and development. Cambridge, MA: Cambridge University Press.

18. Boix, C. (2003). Democracy and Redistribution. Cambridge, MA; Cambridge University Press.

19. Lipset, S. M. (1959). Some Social requisites of democracy: Economic development and political Legitimacy. Bobbs-Merrill.

20. Weiner, M. & Ozbudun, E. Eds (1987). Competitive elections in developing countries. Durham, NC; Duke University Press.

21 Armijo, L.E. (2001). *Financial Globalization and Democracy in Emerging Markets.* New York: Palgrave, p.34

22. Organski, A.F.K. (1973). The stages of political development. New York: Alfred A. Knopt.

23. Heller, P. Rueschemeyer, D. & Snyder, R. (2009).Dependency and Development in a Globalized World: Looking Back and Forward. St Comp .Int. Dev.44.pp. 287-295.

Chapter 11: Development and its Indicators

1. Brinkman, R.L. (1995). Economic Growth versus Economic Development: Towards a Conceptual Clarification. Journal of Economic Issues, Volume 29(4), pp.1171-1188.

2. Greenwood, D., Daphne, T. & Holt, R. (2008). Institutional and ecological economics: The role of technology and institution in economic development. Journal of Economic Issues, 42 (2), 445-450.

3. Smith, S.C. (1997).Case Studies in Economic Development, 2nd Ed. New York: Addison Wesley Longman.

4. Hosseini, H. (2003).Why Development is more complex Than Growth: clarifying some confusions. Review of social economy, LXI (1), pp.93-110.

5. World Bank (1992). World Development Report. New York: Oxford Press.

6. Smith, S.C. (1997).Case Studies in Economic Development, 2nd Ed. New York: Addison Wesley Longman.

7. UNDP (2009). United Nations Development Program, Human Development

Report, 2009. New York: Oxford Press.
8. Ibid.
9. UNDP (2010). United Nations Development Program, Human Development Report, 2010. New York: Oxford Press.

Chapter 12: Internal factors constraining development in Nigeria
1. Brown, W. (2006). The Commission for Africa: results and prospects for the West's Africa policy. *Journal of Modern African Studies,* 44, 3 (2006), pp. 349–374.
2. Acemoglu, D. Johnson, S. & Robinson, J.A. (2001). The colonial origins of comparative development: An empirical investigation. *American Economic Review,* Volume 91, 1369-1401.
3. Moss, T.J Ramachandran, V; & Shah, M.K. (2004) Is Africa's Skepticism of foreign Capital Justified? Evidence from East Africa Firm Survey Data. *Center for Global Development* Working Paper 41.
4. Alence, R. (2004). Political institutions and development governance in Sub-Saharan Africa. *Journal of Modern African Studies, 42* (2), 163-187.
5. Ibid.
6. Ibid.
7. Sandbrook, R. (1985). The Politics of Africa's Economic Stagnation. New York: Press Syndicate, Cambridge University Press.
8. Herbst, J. (1990).The structural adjustment of politics in Africa. *World Development,* volume 18(7), pp. 949-958.
9. Davis, J.H. & Ruhe, J.A. (2003) Perception of country corruption: antecedents and outcomes. *Journal of Business Ethics,* Volume 43(4), pp.275.
10. Ibid.
11. Ibid.
12. Ibid.
13. Geo-JaJa, M. A. & Mangum, G. L. (2000). The Foreign Corrupt Practices Act's Consequences for U.S. Trade: The Nigerian Example. *Journal of Business Ethics,* Volume 24 (3). Part 1, pp. 245-256.
14. Mosley, P. (2004) Institutions and Politics in a Lewis-Type Growth Model. *The Manchester School.* Volume 72(6).
15. Casson, M., Giusta, D. & Kambhampati, U.S. (2010). Formal and Informal and Development. *World Development,* Volume 38(2), .137-141.
16. Levin, R. (2005). Law, endowments and property rights. *Journal of economic Perspectives,* Volume 19(3).
17. De Soto, H. (2000). *The mystery of capital: Why capitalism triumphs in the West and fails everywhere else.* New York: Basic Books.
18. Ibid.

CHAPTER 13: The Modernization Model: a pathway to Development
1. Wang, J. (2009). Some Reflections on Modernization Theory and Globalization Theory. Chinese Studies in History, Volume 43 (1), pp.72-98.
2. Yuan, P. (2009) Modernization Theory. Chinese studies in History, Volume 43(1), pp.37-45
3. Ibid.
4. Ibid.

5. Ibid.
6. Ibid
7. Rostow, W.W. (1960). The Stages of Economic Growth: A Non-Communist Manifesto. Cambridge, MA: The University Press.
8. Cao, F. (2009). Modernization Theory and China's Road to Modernization. Chinese studies in History, Volume 43(1).
9. Ibid
10. Organski, A.F.K. (1973). The Stages of Political Development. New York: Alfred A. Knopt.
11. Ibid.
12. USAID Policy (1991). Democracy and Governance. Washington, DC
13. Cao, F. (2009). Modernization Theory and China's Road to Modernization. Chinese studies in History, Volume 43(1).
14. Ibid.
15. Ibid.
16. Shie, V.H. & Meer, C. D. (2010).The Rise of Knowledge in Dependency Theory: The Experience of India and Taiwan. Review of Radical Political Economics. 42(1), pp.81-99.
17. Ibid.
18. Cao, F. (2009). Modernization Theory and China's Road to Modernization. Chinese studies in History, Volume 43(1).
19. Ibid.
20. Ibid.
21. Wallerstein, I (2004). A World-system perspective on the Social sciences. British Journal of Sociology, volume 61, pp.167-177.

Chapter 14: Genuine Electoral Competition: A force for Development

1. Imoh, c. (2012). The Relationship of Electoral Competition and presidential leadership performance: The case of Nigeria. Ph.D. Dissertation. ProQuest Dissertation & Thesis: Full Text Database (Order Number UMI 3543356).
2. Ibid
3. LeVan, A. (2007). *Dictators, democrats and development in Nigeria. A PhD Dissertation,* University of California, San Diego. AAT 3283913.
4. Tvinnereim, E. M. (2004). *Democratic contestation, accountability and citizen satisfaction in German states.* Paper presented at the annual Meeting of The Midwest Political Science Association, Palmar House Hilton, Chicago, Illinois.
5. Ikpe, U. B. (2009). The impact of manipulated re-elections on accountability and legitimacy of democratic regimes in Africa: Observations from Nigeria, Zambia and Kenya. *African Journal of Political Science and International Relations*, *3(7),* pp. 300-310.
6. LeVan, A. (2007). *Dictators, democrats and development in Nigeria. A PhD Dissertation,* University of California, San Diego. AAT 3283913.
7. Ibid.
8. Tvinnereim, E. M. (2004). *Democratic contestation, accountability and citizen satisfaction in German states.* Paper presented at the annual Meeting of The Midwest Political Science Association, Palmar House Hilton, Chicago, Illinois.

9. Chan, S. (1997). Democracy and Inequality: Tracing welfare spending in Singapore, Taiwan, and South Korea. In Inequality, democracy, and economic Development. Ed. Midlarsky, M. I. Cambridge: Cambridge University Press.

10. Beer, C. & Mitchell, N.J. (2004). Democracy and human rights in the Mexican state: Elections or Social Capital? *International Studies Quarterly, 48*, 293-312.

Chapter 15: Foreign Direct Investment: A tool for Development

1. Chen, E.K.Y. (2005). Teaching and Learning Development Economics: Retrospect and Prospect. Journal of Economic Education, Vol. 36(3).

2. Ghosh, M. & Wang W. (2009).Does FDI Accelerate Economic Growth? The OECD Experience Based on Panel Data Estimates for the Period 1980-2004.Global Economy Journal, Volume 9(4).

3. De Mello, L.R. (1997) Foreign Direct Investment in Developing Countries and Growth: A selective Survey. *Journal of Development Studies,* Volume 34(1), pp.1-34.

4. Romer, P. (1993). Idea gaps and object gaps in economic development. *Journal of Monetary Economics,* Volume 32(3).

5. Kinda, T. (2010). Investment Climate and FDI in Developing Countries: Firm Level Evidence. World Development, Vol. 38(4), pp.498-513, p. 498.

6. Romer, P. (1993). Idea gaps and object gaps in economic development. *Journal of Monetary Economics,* Volume 32(3).

7. Asiedu, E. (2002). On the Determinants of Foreign Direct Investment to Developing Countries: Is Africa Different. *World Development,* Volume 30(1), pp.107-119.

8. Ghosh, M. & Wang W. (2009).Does FDI Accelerate Economic Growth? The OECD Experience Based on Panel Data Estimates for the Period 1980-2004.Global Economy Journal, Volume 9(4).

9. Carcovic, M. & Levine, R. (2002). Does Foreign Direct Investment Accelerate Economic Growth? Department of Business Finance, University of Minnesota, *Working paper series*

10. Lim, E. (2001). Determinants of and the Relation Between. Foreign Direct Investment and Growth: A summary of the Recent Literature. *IMF working paper,* No WP/01/175 pp.1-28.

11. Ibid.

12. Ibid.

13. Ghosh, M. & Wang W. (2009).Does FDI Accelerate Economic Growth? The OECD Experience Based on Panel Data Estimates for the Period 1980-2004.Global Economy Journal, Volume 9(4).

14. Ibid.

15. Asiedu, E. (2004) Policy reform and foreign direct investment in Africa: absolute progress but relative decline. *Development Policy Review,* Volume 22(4), pp.41-48

16. Ibid.

17. Ibid.

18. Ibid.

19. World Bank (2004). *World Development Indicators*. Washington, DC: World Bank

20. Asiedu, E. (2004) Policy reform and foreign direct investment in Africa: absolute progress but relative decline. *Development Policy Review,* Volume 22(4), pp.41-48

21. Vijayakumar, J. Rasheed A. & Tondkar, R. l (2006). Foreign Direct Investment and Evaluation of Country Risk: an Empirical Investigation. *The Multinational Business Review,* Volume17 (3). Pp.181-203.

22. Asiedu, E. (2002). On the Determinants of Foreign Direct Investment to Developing Countries: Is Africa Different. *World Development,* Volume 30(1), pp.107-119.

23. Balasubramanyam, V.N; Salisu, M. & Sapsford, D. (1996). Foreign Direct Investment and growth in EP and IS countries. *The Economic Journal,* Volume 106, pp.92-105.

24. Cao, F. (2009). Modernization Theory and China's Road to Modernization. Chinese studies in History, Volume 43(1).

25. Morisset, J. (2000) Foreign Direct Investment in Africa: Policies Also Matter. *Transnational corporation*, Volume 9(2), pp107-125.

Chapter 16: Primary Factors of Foreign Direct Investment

1. Kinda, T. (2010). Investment Climate and FDI in Developing Countries: Firm Level Evidence. World Development, Volume 38(4), pp.498-513.

2. Ibid.

3. Ibid.

4. Click, R.W. (2005). Financial and Political risks in US direct foreign investment. *Journal of International Studies*, volume 36, pp. 559-575.

5. Moody, A. & Srinivasan, k. (1998). Japanese and U.S. Firms as Foreign: Do They March to the same tune. Canadian *Journal of Economics*, Volume 31.

6. Vijayakumar, J. Rasheed A. & Tondkar, R. l (2006). Foreign Direct Investment and Evaluation of Country Risk: an Empirical Investigation. *The Multinational Business Review,* Volume17 (3). Pp.181-203.

7. Asiedu, E. (2002). On the Determinants of Foreign Direct Investment to Developing Countries: Is Africa Different. *World Development,* Volume 30(1), pp.107-119.

8. Fedderke, J. (2001). Growth and institutions. *Journal of international Development,* Volume 13(6).

9. Vijayakumar, J. Rasheed A. & Tondkar, R. l (2006). Foreign Direct Investment and Evaluation of Country Risk: an Empirical Investigation. *The Multinational Business Review,* Volume17 (3). Pp. 181-203.

10. Balls, D., McCulloch, W.H., Franz, P.L., Geringer, J.M., &Minor, M.S. (2005).International Business: *The Challenge of Global Competition*. New York: The McGraw-Hill Companies, p. 70.

11. Ibid, p. 52).

12. ViewsWire, Nigeria (2007). *Risk Briefing: Nigeria*. Country Profiles and Economic Data Web site.

13. Fedderke, J. (2001). Growth and institutions. *Journal of international Development,* Volume 13(6).

14. Globerman, S. & Shapiro, D. (2003). Governance Infrastructure and US foreign direct Investment. *Journal of international Business studies,* Volume 34(1), pp.19-39.

15. Farrell, D, Remes, J.K. & Sculz, H. (2004). The truth about foreign direct investment in emerging markets. *The Mckinsey Quarterly,* volume 1, pp. 25-35.

16. World Economic Forum (2008). *The Global Competitiveness Report,* 2008-2009.New York: Macmillian.

Chapter 17: The Trend of FDI Inflow to Nigeria

1. Asiedu, E. (2004) Policy reform and foreign direct investment in Africa: absolute progress but relative decline. *Development Policy Review,* Volume 22(4), pp.41-48
2. Ibid.
3. Nonnenberg, M. & Mendonca (2004). The determinants of Direct Foreign Investment in Developing countries. *Transnational Corporation*, Volume 13(1)
4. Chen, E.K.Y. (2005). Teaching and Learning Development Economics: Retrospect and Prospect. Journal of Economic Education, Volume 36(3).
5. Asiedu, E. (2004) Policy reform and foreign direct investment in Africa: absolute progress but relative decline. *Development Policy Review,* Volume 22(4), pp.41-48.
6. Basu, A. & Srinivasan, K. (2002) Foreign Direct Investment in Africa. *IMF Working Paper*, WP/02/61.
7. Ibid.
8. Morisset, J. (2000) Foreign Direct Investment in Africa: Policies Also Matter. *Transnational corporation*, Volume 9(2), pp107-125.
9. Basu, A. & Srinivasan, K. (2002) Foreign Direct Investment in Africa. *IMF Working Paper*, WP/02/61.
10. United Nations Center for Trade and Development (UNCTD). *Foreign Direct Investment in Africa: Performance and Potential*. New York: United Nations Publication.
11. Basu, A. & Srinivasan, K. (2002) Foreign Direct Investment in Africa. *IMF Working Paper*, WP/02/61.
12. Asiedu, E. (2002). On the Determinants of Foreign Direct Investment to Developing Countries: Is Africa Different. *World Development,* Volume 30(1), pp. 107-119.
13. Ibid.
14. Morisset, J. (2000) Foreign Direct Investment in Africa: Policies Also Matter. *Transnational corporation*, Volume 9(2), pp107-125.
15. Basu, A. & Srinivasan, K. (2002) Foreign Direct Investment in Africa. *IMF Working Paper*, WP/02/61.
16. Ibid.

Chapter 18: Constraints to Foreign Direct Investment into Nigeria

1. Kinda, T. (2010). Investment Climate and FDI in Developing Countries: Firm Level Evidence. World Development, Volume 38(4), pp.498-513.
2. Ibid.
3. Moody, A. & Srinivasan, k. (1998). Japanese and U.S. Firms as Foreign: Do They March to the same tune. Canadian *Journal of Economics*, Volume 31.
4. Suliman, A.H. & Mollick, A.V. (2009). Human Capital Development, war and Foreign Direct investment in sub-Saharan Africa. *Oxford Development Studies,* volume (1), pp.4761.
5. Balls, D., McCulloch, W.H., Franz, P.L., Geringer, J.M., &Minor, M.S. (2005). International Business: *The Challenge of Global Competition*. New York; The McGraw-Hill Companies, p.300.
6. Basu, A. & Srinivasan, K. (2002) Foreign Direct Investment in Africa. *IMF Working Paper*, WP/02/61
7. Kinda, T. (2010). Investment Climate and FDI in Developing Countries: Firm Level

Evidence. World Development, Volume 38(4), pp.498-513.

8. Asiedu, E. (2002). On the Determinants of Foreign Direct Investment to Developing Countries: Is Africa Different. *World Development,* Volume 30(1), pp.107-119.

9. Kinda, T. (2010). Investment Climate and FDI in Developing Countries: Firm Level Evidence. World Development, Volume 38(4), pp.498-513.

10. ViewsWire, Nigeria (2007). *Risk Briefing: Nigeria.* Country Profiles and Economic Data Web site.

11. Ibid.

12. Asiedu, E. (2002). On the Determinants of Foreign Direct Investment to Developing Countries: Is Africa Different. *World Development,* Volume 30(1), pp.107-119, p. 18.

13. Sachs, J. & Sievers, S. (1998). *FDI in Africa.* Africa Competitiveness Report. Geneva: World   Economic Forum.

14. Howell, L.D. & Chaddick, B. (1994) Models of Political risk for foreign investment and trade: An assessment of three approaches. *Columbia journal of World Business,* 71-91, p.71.

15. Basu, A. & Srinivasan, K. (2002) Foreign Direct Investment in Africa. *IMF Working Paper*, WP/02/61.

16. Ibid.

17. Rotberg, R. (2007). *Governance and leadership in Africa*, Broomal, PA: Mason Crest Publishers.

18. International Finance Corporation (2014). Doing Business Report: Starting a business. Retrieved from www.ifc.org.

19. Geo-JaJa, M. A. & Mangum, G. L. (2000). The Foreign Corrupt Practices Act's Consequences for U.S. Trade: The Nigerian Example. *Journal of Business Ethics,* Volume 24 (3). Part 1, pp. 245-256.

20. Nonnenberg, M. & Mendonca (2004). The determinants of Direct Foreign Investment in Developing countries. *Transnational Corporation*, Volume 13(1)

21. Asiedu, E. (2002). On the Determinants of Foreign Direct Investment to Developing Countries: Is Africa Different. *World Development,* Volume 30(1), pp.107-119.

22. Noorbakhsh, F., Paloni, A. & Youssef, A. (2001). Human capital and FDI inflows to developing countries: new empirical evidence. *World Development,* Volume 29, pp. 1593-1610.

23. Shie, V.H. & Meer, C. D. (2010).The Rise of Knowledge in Dependency Theory: The Experience of India and Taiwan. *Review of Radical Political Economics*. Vol. 42(1), pp. 81-99.

24. Moody, A. & Srinivasan, k. (1998). Japanese and U.S. Firms as Foreign: Do They March to the same tune. Canadian *Journal of Economics*, Volume 31.

Chapter 19: Corruption: The Elephant in the Room

1. Quah, J.S. (2003). Curbing Corruption in Asia. Singapore: Eastern Universities.

2. Transparency International (2010). *Corruption perception index*. Berlin: Transparency International.

3. Rotberg, R. (2004). Strengthening Africa leadership. *Foreign Affairs, 83* (4), 14-18.

4. Obama, B.H. (2006).An honest Government-A hopeful future. Speech delivered at the University of Nairobi, Kenya, on August 8th2006.

5. Davis, J.H. & Ruhe, J.A. (2003) Perception of country corruption: antecedents and

outcomes. *Journal of Business Ethics,* Vol. 43(4), pp.275

6. Davis, J.H. & Ruhe, J.A. (2003) Perception of country corruption: antecedents and outcomes. *Journal of Business Ethics,* Volume 43(4).

7. Ibid.

8. ViewsWire, Nigeria (2010). *Risk briefing: Nigeria.* Country Profiles and Economic Data Web site.

9. Gberevbie, D.E. (2009). Democracy and the future of the Nigerian State. *Journal of Social Development in Africa, 24*(1), 165-191, p. 172.

Chapter 20: Creating the Environment for Foreign Direct Investment

1. Suliman, A.H. & Mollick, A.V. (2009). Human Capital Development, war and Foreign Direct investment in sub-Saharan Africa. *Oxford Development Studies,* volume (1), pp.4761.

2. Mozaffar, S. (2005). Negotiating Independence in Mauritius. *International Negotiation, 10*(2), 263–291, 264.

3. Basu, A. & Srinivasan, K. (2002) Foreign Direct Investment in Africa. *IMF Working Paper,* WP/02/61.

4. Mozaffar, S. (2005). Negotiating Independence in Mauritius. *International Negotiation, 10*(2), 263–291.

5. Asiedu, Elizabeth (2006). Foreign Direct Investment: The Role of Natural Resources, Market Size, Government Policy, Institutions and Political Instability. *World Economy,* Volume 29(1), pp.67-72.

6. Morisset, J. (2000) Foreign Direct Investment in Africa: Policies Also Matter. *Transnational corporation,* Volume 9(2), pp107-125.

7. Ibid.

8. Pigato, M. (2001). *The foreign Direct Investment Environment in Africa.* The World Bank: Africa Region Working paper series 15.

9. Lee, C. & Wilhelm, W. (2010). On Integrating Theories of International Economics in the Strategic Planning of global supply chains and facility location. *Int. J. production Economics,* Volume 124, pp. 225-240.

10. Ibid.

11. Asiedu, E. (2004) Policy reform and foreign direct investment in Africa: absolute progress but relative decline. *Development Policy Review,* Volume 22(4), pp.41-48.

12. Lim, E. (2001). Determinants of and the Relation Between. Foreign Direct Investment and Growth: A summary of the Recent Literature. *IMF working paper,* No WP/01/175 pp.1-28.

13. Euromonitor International (2006). *Tanzania: Country Profile.* Retrieved from Country Profiles and Economic Data web site

14. Levy, B. (2006) Emerging Countries, Regionalization, and World Trade Global *Economy Journal 6* (4) 29-31.

15. Ibid, p. 2.

16. Asiedu, Elizabeth (2006). Foreign Direct Investment: The Role of Natural Resources, Market Size, Government Policy, Institutions and Political Instability. *World Economy,* Volume 29(1), pp.67-72.

Chapter 21: The Use and Benefits of Export Processing Zones

1. Balls, D., McCulloch, W.H., Franz, P.L., Geringer, J.M., &Minor, M.S. (2005).

International Business: *The Challenge of Global Competition.* New York: The McGraw-Hill Companies, p.70.

2. Ibid.

3. Ibid.

4. Shie, V.H. & Meer, C. D. (2010).The Rise of Knowledge in Dependency Theory: The Experience of India and Taiwan. *Review of Radical Political Economics.* Vol. 42 (1), pp. 81-99.

5. Ibid.

Chapter 22: Policies to Attract Foreign Direct Investments into Export Processing Zones

1. Basu, A. & Srinivasan, K. (2002) Foreign Direct Investment in Africa. *IMF Working Paper*, WP/02/61.

2. Armitage, T. (2007). Mauritius: Economic and Risks. *Mauritius Country Monitor 57*(1), 49-54, p. 50

3 World Tourism Organizations (2004). Tourism market trends. Retrieved from www.Unwto.org.

Chapter 23: Macro- and Micro- reforms

 1. Krugman, P.R. (1994). The Myth of Asian's Miracle. *Foreign Affairs*, Volume 73, pp. 62-78.

2. Friedman, T. (2005). *The World is Flat: A brief History of the Twenty-First Century.* New York: Farrar, Staus, and Girous.

3. Ibid, p. 317).

4. Ibid, p. 318).

5. International Finance Corporation (IFC, 2014). Doing Business Report: Business Reforms. Retrieved from www.ifc.org.

6. International Finance Corporation (2014). Doing Business Report: Starting a business. Retrieved from www.ifc.org.

7. Ibid

8. International Finance Corporation (2014). Doing Business Report: Enforcing a contract. Retrieved from www.ifc.org.

9. International Finance Corporation (2014). Doing Business Report: Getting credit. Retrieved from www.ifc.org.

10. Ibid

11. International Finance Corporation (2014). Doing Business Report: Business Reforms. Retrieved from www.ifc.org.

12. Landes, D. (1999). *The Wealth and Poverty of Nations. New York: W.W. Norton & Company.*

13. Friedman, T. (2005). *The World is Flat: A brief History of the Twenty-First Century.* New York: Farrar, Staus, and Girous

14. Kemmelmeier, Markus; Eugene Burnstein; Krum Krunov; Petia Genkova; Chie Kanagara; Mathew Hirshberg; Hans-Peter Erb; Grazyna Wieczorkowska and Kimberly Noels. (2003). Individualism, collectivism, and authoritarianism in seven societies. *Journal of Cross-Cultural Psychology* 34(3): 304–322.

15. Javidan Mansour and Robert J. House, (2001). Cultural Acumen for the Global

manager: Lessons from GLOBE project. *Organizational Dynamics, 29*(4), 289-305.

16. Hofstede, G. (1980). *Culture's Consequences: International Differences in Work-Related Values*, Beverly Hills, CA: Sage.

17. Griffith, D.; M. Hu, & J. Ryans, Jr, (2000). Process Standardization across intra- and inter-cultural relationships. Journal of International Business Studies, 31(2), 303-325.

Chapter 24: Instituting a Well-defined Private Property System

1. Reed, O.L, Shedd, P.J., Morehead, J.W., & Corley, R.N. (2005). The legal & Regulatory environment of business. New York: McGraw-Hill Irwin, p. 178.

2. Ibid, p. 179.

3. Ibid, p. 188.

4. Ibid, p. 178.

5. Casson, M., Giusta, D. & Kambhampati, U.S. (2010). Formal and informal and development. *World Development, 38*(2), 137-141.

6. Hernando De Soto (2001, p.11). The mystery of capital: Why capitalism triumphs in the West and fails everywhere else. New York: Basic Books.

7. De Soto, H. (2000). *The mystery of capital: Why capitalism triumphs in the West and fails everywhere else.* New York: Basic Books.

8. Ibid.

9. Reed, O.L, Shedd, P.J., Morehead, J.W., & Corley, R.N. (2005). The legal & Regulatory environment of business. New York: McGraw-Hill Irwin, p. 181

10. Ibid, p. 182

11. Ibid.

Chapter 25: Technological Reforms for Take-off

1. Rostow, W.W. (1960). The Stages of Economic Growth: A Non-Communist Manifesto. Cambridge, MA: The University Press.

2. Ibid.

3. Ibid.

4. Ibid.

5. Ibid.

6. Ibid.

7. Friedman, T. (2005 Friedman, T. (2005). *The World is Flat: A brief History of the Twenty-First Century. New York: Farrar, Staus, and Girous*

www.ingramcontent.com/pod-product-compliance
Lightning Source LLC
Chambersburg PA
CBHW050133280326
41933CB00010B/1353